BEING PREZ

BEING PREZ

THE LIFE AND MUSIC OF LESTER YOUNG

DAVE GELLY

OXFORD
UNIVERSITY PRESS

2007

Oxford University Press, Inc., publishes works that further
Oxford University's objective of excellence
in research, scholarship, and education.

Oxford   New York
Auckland   Cape Town   Dar es Salaam   Hong Kong   Karachi
Kuala Lumpur   Madrid   Melbourne   Mexico City   Nairobi
New Delhi   Shanghai   Taipei   Toronto

With offices in
Argentina   Austria   Brazil   Chile   Czech Republic   France   Greece
Guatemala   Hungary   Italy   Japan Poland   Portugal   Singapore
South Korea   Switzerland   Thailand   Turkey   Ukraine   Vietnam

First published by Equinox Publishing Ltd., Unit 6,
The Village, 101 Amies St., London, SW11 2JW, 2007.

Published by Oxford University Press, Inc.
198 Madison Avenue, New York, New York 10016

www.oup.com

Oxford is a registered trademark of Oxford University Press

Library of Congress Cataloging-in-Publication Data
Gelly, Dave.
Being Prez : the life and music of Lester Young / Dave Gelly.
    p.   cm.
Includes bibliographical references, discography, and index.
ISBN 978-0-19-533477-7
1. Young, Lester, 1909–1959.   2. Jazz musicians—United States—Biography. I. Title.
ML419.Y7G43 2007
788.7'165092—dc22   2007029024

Typesetting by CA Typesetting Ltd., www.publisherservices.co.uk

9 8 7 6 5 4 3 2 1

Printed in the United States of America
on acid-free paper

For Annie

Let us steadily remember, Gentlemen, that the true test of genius lies in its durability; in its strength to withstand age and weather and vicissitudes of taste, to emerge from disrepute and neglect, to submit to the touch of Time, yet abide ineffaceably itself.

Sir Arthur Quiller-Couch in *Studies in Literature (Second Series)*, 1922

But you take a person like me. I stay by myself, so how do you know anything about me?

Lester Young, interviewed by François Postif, Paris, 1959

contents

preface

In the Pantheon of jazz music, the name of Lester Young ranks with those of Louis Armstrong, Charlie Parker, Miles Davis or John Coltrane. That is to say, he is numbered among the greatest artists in an idiom which played a large part in defining musical sensibility in the twentieth century.

Yet he has remained a curiously elusive figure. Most people with a general interest in cultural matters will at least have heard of Armstrong, Parker *et al.*, but mention of Lester Young is likely to be greeted by blank looks. The reasons for this are not hard to discover. Much of his best work was done as a sideman, under someone else's leadership. His style was subtle and restrained. He was a shy, mild-mannered individual in a thrusting, attention-seeking profession. His career was interrupted at a crucial moment by a disastrous period in the wartime US Army. He was a chronic alcoholic and died young.

And yet, there is no more consistently perfect body of recorded work in jazz than that produced by Lester Young between 1936 and 1941 – with Count Basie's orchestra, with Billie Holiday and with various small groups such as the Kansas City Seven. The elegance and wit of his playing are of an entirely different order from anything previously expressed in jazz. Later, as life's vicissitudes crowded in upon him, the complexion of his playing grew darker and its emotional range more profound. His effect on the art he practised was incalculable, both as a direct stylistic influence and, more generally, as an inspiration to those seeking to renew the jazz language.

Over the years since his death, Lester Young has been the subject of articles, dissertations, discographies, album and CD notes, books, poems and at least one opera (*Prez: A Jazz Opera* by Bernard Cash and Alan Plater, produced and broadcast by BBC2 television, 1985). A substantial list of these can be found following his entry in the *New Grove Dictionary of Jazz*, but special mention should be made of *You Just Fight For Your Life: The Story of Lester Young* and its companion volume *You Got To Be Original, Man! The Music of Lester Young*, both by Frank Büchmann-Møller. The first is an excellent biography, including a quite invaluable chronology of Lester's professional life, and the second an annotated discography. Both books are exemplary and clearly the work of a musician and a scholar. Professor Lewis Porter's book, *Lester Young*, belies its modest size with its wealth of information, musicological analysis and scrupulous technical detail. *Lester Leaps In: The Life and Times of Lester 'Pres' Young*, by Professor Douglas Henry Daniels, is the largest book of all and contains a vast amount of information, especially about Lester's family and cultural background. Indeed, so dense is the detail that the narrative often becomes submerged beneath it.

Anyone proposing to add to this cornucopia is more or less obliged to offer some excuse, and mine is as follows. The biography of a creative artist is of particular interest in so far as the life and the art enlighten one another. The world into which the artist is born, the culture in which he grows and the events of his life determine the form which the art takes, and is of specific interest for that reason. The most illuminating biographies are those in which these elements are presented as a unity, yet in none of the above-mentioned works is this the case. The elements are treated separately and the reader is left to discover any connection there may be between the one and the other. I have endeavoured to bring them together by treating Lester Young's life and art as an indivisible whole. I have also tried to tell the story in a straightforward, chronological manner.

The story of Lester Young presents one particular difficulty, namely that more than half his life was passed in virtual obscurity. Jazz music is preserved in recordings, yet he did not enter a recording studio until the age of twenty-seven and died before the age of fifty. Any account of his early life and career has therefore to be told without reference to examples of his work. The researches of the authors mentioned above have proved invaluable guides to this period and I have had much recourse to them. In addition, I have tried to sketch in the musical world which would have surrounded Lester Young in his early years.

When it came to discussing musical points, I decided against including extracts in musical notation, in the interests of accessibility as much and anything else. Following the aspiration of Samuel Johnson, 'I rejoice to concur with the common reader', and the common reader does not necessarily read music. My main aim has been to communicate some of the delight which Lester Young's music has brought me, and if possible to share it. As the years pass and the jazz idiom takes on new forms, there is a danger that even great artists will be, if not forgotten, then relegated to the status of revered ancestors and consigned to the museum. Thus, another aim of this book is, in some small way, to rescue Lester's music from what E.P. Thompson called 'the enormous condescension of posterity'.

Besides the authors mentioned above, I am grateful for the help of Stan Britt, Michael Brooks, Russell Davies, Nick Gold, Malcolm Laycock, David Nathan (of the UK National Jazz Archive), Roy Oakshott, Brian Priestley, Alyn Shipton and the mysterious GaraiJAN@aol.com, who is the complete enquire-within on all matters appertaining to saxophone mouthpieces, reeds etc. My thoughts on Lester's later work were concentrated by contributing notes to the Complete Verve Studio Sessions, released in 1999. I am grateful to Ben Young and Bryan Koniarz, of Verve's New York office, for providing me with that opportunity.

As to the spelling of Lester's honorific – should it be 'Pres' or 'Prez'? – I have seen it spelt both ways. Having to decide, I plumped for the latter, mainly because that is how it is pronounced.

Unless otherwise stated, the musical commentaries are entirely my own, based upon more than half a century of listening and some practical acquaintance with the tenor saxophone and its vagaries.

Dave Gelly
London, 2007

BEING PREZ

1 'I just loved that music'

Woodville, in Wilkinson County, Mississippi, is the birthplace of two famous Americans – Jefferson Davis (1808–89), President of the Confederacy, and Lester Young (1909–1959), saxophonist. Apart from their place of birth, they seem to have had only one thing in common, namely that they both served time in jail. In the year in which Lester Young was born, Woodville and its environs boasted a population of 2,500, with blacks outnumbering whites by almost two to one. Racial segregation was rigidly enforced, disputes might be settled with a bullet, and lynchings were not unknown. At around the time of Lester's birth, on 27 August 1909, a local election was held, during which the National Guard were called in to quell a riot. In other words, just another quiet, hospitable Southern town.

If Lester ever felt nostalgia for the antebellum charms of Woodville he never mentioned it. After his first few weeks in the world he was removed from the town and rarely saw it again. His family home was in New Orleans, more specifically in Algiers, on the south bank of the Mississippi, opposite the famous French Quarter. It was his mother's parents who lived in Woodville, and it was with them that she stayed when she was expecting her first child. As Lester explained it towards the end of his life, in his hip, laconic fashion: 'My mother was scared, you know, that type, so she wanted to go back home in case something happened... So after I was straight and she made it and everything was cool, then she takes me to New Orleans and we lived in Algiers.'[1]

Lester's mother, Lizetta, whose maiden name was Johnson, was aged twenty when she gave birth to Lester. She was of light complexion and probably descended from the free, mixed-race *gens de couleur libres* who had formed a distinct stratum of Louisiana society before the civil war. Her husband, Willis Handy Young, aged thirty-seven in 1909, was a man with a powerful drive towards self-improvement and success. Born in Thibodaux, Louisiana, the son of a blacksmith, he learned his father's trade before gaining admission to Tuskegee Institute, the school in Alabama established by the great pioneer of Negro education, Booker T. Washington.

There he studied a variety of subjects, including history, but specialized in music. During vacations he returned to his family home and worked at his father's forge. By the time he graduated, Willis Young (universally known as 'Billy') had a working knowledge of most musical instruments – brass, reed, percussion, keyboard – and a particular mastery of the cornet.

Figure 1. 1910. Lester, age one, with his adored mother, Lizetta. (Frank Driggs collection)

After graduating, Billy Young became a teacher in New Orleans, supplementing his meagre salary by giving private music lessons, playing the cornet and eventually becoming a bandleader. There are few reliable records of his early life, but his main occupation seems to have fluctuated between teaching and performing for quite some time. He married Lizetta, who had been one of his private music students, in 1908. They settled in Algiers, but he was away from home a great deal. For a while, apparently, he was the principal of a school in Bogalusa, about 60 miles north of New Orleans. At other times he toured as a musician. Whatever the case, his visits home were so infrequent that he seems to have played very little part in his children's early upbringing. There were three of them – Willis Lester, Irma Cornelia (born 1912) and Leonidas Raymond (born 1917).

Whenever Lester Young spoke about the first ten years of his life, his memories were always happy ones and they mostly concerned music. This is hardly surprising, considering his latent musicality and the time and place in which he found himself. New Orleans at the start of the twentieth century was unlike any other American city. France and Spain had both owned it in the past, and its history had made it racially diverse, culturally cosmopolitan and strongly Roman Catholic. Geography had made it sub-tropical and many people spoke a creole patois of French and English. In some ways it would have been more suited to the shores of the Mediterranean than the banks of the Mississippi. Most important of all, New Orleans was widely acknowledged to be the most musical city in America. No social event, no matter how trivial, could take place without its appropriate musical accompaniment. In their memoirs, veteran New Orleans-born musicians, such as Louis Armstrong and Jelly Roll Morton, reel off mind-boggling lists of balls, banquets, parties, marriages, funerals, first communions and picnics beside Lake Pontchartrain. The climate ensured that most activities took place out of doors, so that the common air was filled with music.

Danny Barker, the New Orleans guitarist, born in the same year as Lester Young, recalled: 'A bunch of us kids, playing, would suddenly hear sounds. It was a phenomenon, like the Aurora Borealis maybe. The sounds of men playing would be so clear, but we wouldn't be sure where they were coming from. So we'd start trotting, start running – 'It's this way! It's that way!... That music could come on you at any time like that.'[2] Lester himself might have been one of those kids. He certainly remembered the same scene: 'Every time they'd start to play, anything I was doing, they start playing some music – Boom! I'd run there... I just loved that music. I'd be running around till my tongue was hanging out like this.'[3]

He was a sweet-natured, dreamy child who adored his mother and she, in turn, doted on him. He had inherited her light complexion and green, expressive eyes. His hair had a reddish tinge to it. Although he later claimed to have earned his own living from the age of five or six, by selling newspapers, shining shoes and giving out handbills, he said it with none of the tough-kid swagger that usually accompanies such assertions. Quite the reverse. In the next breath he hastened to add: 'But I was a good kid. I would *never* steal'.[4] As an adult he would go to extreme lengths to avoid conflict or unpleasantness of any kind, a trait which seems to have been present from his earliest years.

Lizetta was Billy Young's second wife. How his first marriage ended is not known, but his second probably crumbled under the strain of prolonged absences. The final blow came in 1919, when Billy took up with another woman, Sarah Pilgrim, whom he later married. At around the same time he joined the Hagenback and Wallace Circus as bandleader of its sideshow. When the marriage ended he somehow assumed custody of the children and sent his sister, Mamie, to collect them. 'Mama was at work when she came and got us', Irma recalled. 'She told us she was taking us down for a visit, but when we got in there, Papa got us and he taken us with him wherever he was going.'⁵ They did not see their mother again for at least ten years. However you look at it, this seems more like abduction than custody.

Much has been written about the estimable personal qualities of Willis Handy Young – his unwavering devotion to study and self-advancement, his grim determination to succeed against the odds, his considerable musical gifts, his talent for administration and his dignified conduct under the barely tolerable yoke of Southern racism. But among all these splendid qualities at least one attribute was plainly missing – namely, a tender heart. To take a child away from its mother by means of a trick is a wicked thing to do. When that child is a shy, sensitive little boy with a deep mutual attachment to his mother, it is unforgivable. According to Irma, Lester wept bitterly for a long time afterwards. No doubt Lizetta wept, too.

It is hard to dismiss the assumption that Billy Young wanted to have his children with him in order to train them up eventually as members of his band, the New Orleans Strutters. Now that he had committed himself to the show-business life, he set about creating not simply a band but an entire show built around members of his extended family. He also took on two nephews, William 'Sport' Young and Austin 'Boots' Young, who played saxophones and various other instruments. The term 'sideshow' is somewhat misleading. In the case of Hagenback and Wallace's circus, it was more like a complete and separate production, set up in the form of a minstrel show and housed in its own tent. It included a traditional scene in which the cast sat in a semicircle, cracking jokes, while a chairman (or 'interlocutor') kept – or failed to keep – order. Then there were songs and dances and audience participation, the whole thing preceded by an energetic warm-up routine known as the 'ballyhoo'.

Minstrelsy is scarcely mentioned nowadays. It is written off as an unsavoury episode in popular culture, presumably because the performers appeared in 'blackface' makeup, even the ones whose faces were black already. It must be admitted that minstrelsy pandered to the stereotype of black people held by most whites at the time, in which innocent stupidity contended with low cunning, and music was represented by crude sentimentality or a cheerful, mindless din. Nevertheless, minstrelsy succeeded in fostering high levels of musical, comedic and terpsichorean skill, and in entertaining generations of working-class people, both black and white.

Billy Young, with his commanding presence and teaching background, made a highly effective band director. He trained young players, having first acquired their instruments at a discount, planned the show, hired musicians, chose the music, wrote the arrangements, conducted the band and played the leading role himself. He was good with figures, wrote an impressive letter and could talk the hind leg off a donkey.

As the children grew up they were put to learning the family trade. Lester, being the eldest, was first. He started out playing the drums and, according to his own account, 'I really played them. I could play my ass off. I played them for three years.' But, as generations of drummers have learned to their cost, the drum kit has its drawbacks, the most irksome being its size and the myriad bits and pieces which have to be assembled before a performance and packed away afterwards. When Lester was around thirteen years old, and beginning to take an interest in girls, he found that by the time he had packed his kit away, the prettiest girls had all been spoken for. 'All the other guys got their clarinet cases, trombone cases, trumpet cases and here I am, wiggling around with all this shit!... Carryin' all them drums got to be a real grind. I decided I'd better get me a lighter instrument.'[6]

His father gave him an alto saxophone, and he took to it at once. It has been suggested that the drums were passed on to his little brother. Leonidas, who grew up to be Lee Young, a well-known and successful drummer, would have been only five years old in 1922, when Lester was thirteen, but the drum kit was there and he could have made its acquaintance, even at that tender age. Certainly, it was not long before both Lee and Irma were taking part in the show. Lee was a robust, extrovert little boy, who loved being the centre of attention. He sang and danced and cut capers, dressed in a cute sailor suit and a huge bow tie. Irma sang and danced, too, and when she was big enough, took the part of the lady who was sawn in half. And everyone played at least one instrument. Irma became a very good saxophonist, Lee played the saxophone as well as drums, and even Sarah Young, their stepmother, learned the saxophone and banjo to a competent standard.

Figure 2. 1924. The New Orleans Strutters in Lexington, Kentucky. On left of picture, with baritone saxophone, is Sarah Young (Lester's step-mother). In the centre, holding a trumpet, is Billy Young. To his right, with tenor saxophone and clad in plus-fours, is the fifteen-year-old Lester. The tiny minstrel in the large top hat, behind Billy's left shoulder, may well be the eight-year-old Lee. (Frank Driggs collection)

Throughout its early years, the family band followed a regular touring routine. They would spend roughly half the year with the Hagenback and Wallace circus and the other half touring a circuit of theatres under the auspices of the Theater Owners' Booking Association, a well-known body in its day, commonly referred to by its initials, TOBA. Wags among the performers insisted that the letters stood for 'Tough On Black Asses'. With the circus, all personnel and equipment travelled in specially chartered trains, but when touring the TOBA circuit the performers used regular scheduled rail services or private cars. The progress of the New Orleans Strutters was occasionally eased by the fact that Billy Young was a Freemason, as were many train conductors and Pullman staff. Itineraries were booked well in advance, a necessary precaution with so many companies on the move. The New Orleans Strutters were part of a large network of shows criss-crossing the country in the early decades of the twentieth century, shows such as the famous Rabbit Foot Minstrels, the Bandana Babies and Tolliver's Circus & Musical Extravaganza.

What kind of music did they play, and what did it sound like? We can gain some idea by examining songs popular at the time, from listening to early recordings, dim though they mostly sound today, and from history in general. Songs frequently mentioned by veteran musicians in their reminiscences include 'Margie', 'Way Down Yonder In New Orleans', 'Yes Sir! That's My Baby', 'Last Night On The Old Back Porch' and 'Ja-Da'. This last number is one of many virtually identical songs based on the same sixteen-bar pattern, so common at the time as almost to qualify as an American folk-song. Its variants include 'How Come You Do Me Like You Do?', 'I'm A Ding-Dong Daddy From Dumas', 'Hurry On Down' and any number of mildly salacious items such as 'I Didn't Like It The First Time' and 'She's Got 'Em, She Wears 'Em (She's Got A Pair Of BVDs)'. The single attribute possessed by all these songs is their strong, simple, whistleable melodies.

Traditional minstrelsy was undergoing a transformation at this time, with the sudden popularity of the blues among black audiences. Blues was a southern folk idiom and did not figure in professional entertainment during the earliest years of the twentieth century. Indeed, when Ma Rainey, the singer often called 'Mother of the Blues', began her professional career in 1904, she seems not to have been aware of it. The musicologist John Wesley Work Jr interviewed her toward the end of her life and reported: 'She tells of a girl from the town [in Missouri] who came to the tent one morning and began to sing about the "man" who had left her. The song was so strange and poignant that it attracted much attention. Ma Rainey...learned the song from the visitor and used it soon afterward... The song elicited such response from the audience that it found a special place in her act.'[7] That song was a blues, and Ma Rainey was singing it regularly by about 1910. It became her speciality and the basis of her considerable drawing power. Over the next few years the cadences of the blues began to seep into black entertainment. The sudden burst of popular enthusiasm came in 1920, with the release of the record 'Crazy Blues', sung by Trixie Smith. This was virtually the first phonograph record to be aimed specifically at the African-American public, and its success took everyone by surprise.

With hindsight, we can see that the conditions were absolutely right. We know, for example, that a great northward migration of African-American people was taking place. Industry was expanding at a great rate in the north, offering wages far better than anything available in the rural south. At the same time, a series of disastrous floods, plus the ravages of the boll weevil, had recently brought several southern states to the verge of ruin. Add to this a degree of racial oppression in those same states, which kept most black people in virtual servitude, and the urge to move must have been well-nigh irresistible. Those who moved tended to be young. For the first time in their lives they had a little spare money to spend on enjoyment and modern gadgets such as phonographs. And then along came this record, in an exciting new idiom drawn from their own culture and sung by one of their own. A close parallel would be the rise of reggae in the late 1960s. Estimates of the sales figures vary wildly, but 'Crazy Blues' certainly sold in its tens of thousands, and this was achieved without the aid of radio, which did not yet exist as a public broadcasting medium.

It is possible to catch some flavour of the material and performing style of the time from records by contemporary artists such as Leola 'Coot' Grant and Wesley 'Sox' Wilson ('Come On Coot And Do That Thing', Paramount 1925), Butterbeans and Susie ('He Likes It Slow', Okeh 1926) and Alberta Hunter with the Red Onion Jazz Babies ('Cake Walking Babies From Home', Gennett 1924). This last piece has incidental relevance, since its composer, Clarence Williams, had been one of Billy Young's private music pupils, back in New Orleans. As well as being a prolific songwriter, Williams achieved considerable prominence in the world of black popular music during the 1920s, as pianist, bandleader, talent scout and recording director – in effect, a kind of prehistoric Quincy Jones. His work is very much of its time, but several of his songs, including 'Squeeze Me' and 'Baby, Won't You Please Come Home', are still performed to this day.

Such was the musical milieu in which Lester Young passed the second decade of his life, the decade in which he became a musician. He learned his craft through practising two musical forms, the American popular song and the blues, and these would provide the sole material of his art for the rest of his career. It was soon discovered that he possessed a natural affinity for the saxophone, along with an immensely quick ear and a highly retentive memory. In a remarkably short time he seems to have caught up with his older cousins, Sport and Boots, in instrumental technique, and then overtaken them. His sister, Irma, is reputed to have done the same in her turn. Lester, in later life, certainly spoke admiringly of her abilities.

It often happens that people with exceptionally good ears find learning to read music a bore. If you can play something perfectly after hearing it once, why bother to sweat through sight-reading exercises? Jazz history is littered with great musicians whose reading abilities were either limited or non existent. As beginners, many of them succeeded in fooling their teachers by listening to a piece once, remembering it and reproducing what they had heard. Fats Waller, for instance, got away with this for several years as a child. If one hearing proved insufficient he would turn a pair of wide, soulful eyes on his piano teacher with the words, 'Oh, Miss, that was so pretty! Won't you please play it one more time?' Lester Young, too, got away with the ear-and-memory trick for a while, but Billy Young was a tough nut and invulnerable to childish wiles, however charming. He set a trap for Lester. He wrote out a passage on a blackboard then played it over, with several departures from the written notes. Lester reproduced what he had just heard, not what was on the board, and the cat was out of the bag. As a punishment, he was banished from the band until he had learned to read. The humiliation was particularly bitter because people had begun to treat him as something special, a little star in the making. ('How did he learn to play all that stuff?' 'Oh, man, he learned it from his daddy. He knows how to play 'em all!')[8]

Lester had always been a sensitive child and he took the banishment very hard. The episode stayed with him for the rest of his life. He would bring it up whenever the talk took a reminiscent turn, the last occasion probably being a conversation recorded in Paris, a few weeks before his death: 'Now, you know, my heart was broke, you dig, and I went in crying my little teardrops and I was thinking, I'll come back and catch 'em, if that's the way they want it. So I went away and I learned to read the music, still by myself, and I came back in the band and played this music and shit...and everything was great...and I showed them!'[9]

The relationship between father and son was never an easy one. Billy Young was a hard taskmaster, stern and unbending. Many years later, one of his grandchildren aptly summed him up as 'absolutely the autocrat of all time'.[10] Lester's languid, semi-detached manner drove him to distraction, but at the same time he was proud of his eldest son's evident talent. According to Lee, Irma and everyone else who has spoken on the subject, Lester was clearly the apple of his father's eye, but Billy Young would have died rather than admit it. Instead, he stuck rigidly to his code of rewards and punishments, the latter featuring liberal use of the strap. Lester, with his horror of aggression or harsh words, simply could not accept this, and his solution was to run away. He did it quite regularly, beginning at the age of eleven or twelve, and nobody knew where he went or how he survived. He would eventually reappear and carry on as though nothing had occurred. This proved to be a very effective form of passive resistance, forcing his father to accept him back on his own terms and restoring tranquillity. Until the next time.

Lee Young watched all this with the eyes of a shrewd child.

> Greasy Jim, that was the name of his razor strap, you know. Well,
> I would go and get it and just stand up there and really take mine,
> but you couldn't do that to Lester, because he would leave home. He
> would run away if you hit him... They needed to beat me....because I

was stubborn, very, very stubborn… Lester, I think talking to him would have done it for him… Never would have done it for me… When he would come back, everything would be okay. He never did question him, never questioned him. And you're talking about a time when men really would question their kids… Parents learn, or they should learn, that if you have three or four kids, you cannot deal with all of them in the same manner. They all have different temperaments.[11]

The number of miles covered by the Young family band in its travels almost beggars belief. In 1924 alone, the year of Lester's fifteenth birthday, the itinerary stretched from Seattle, Washington, to Pensacola, Florida – a distance of over three thousand miles. In those early days, however, the bulk of the band's work was concentrated in the southern states. Even though they stuck together and looked out for one another, members of the band and the other black show-people lived constantly under the shadow of segregation and institutional racism. Their position was particularly delicate because their itinerant occupation made them permanent outsiders, and therefore ready targets of suspicion or gratuitous assault. On at least one occasion Lester, together with one of his cousins, had to run for his life from a gang of white ruffians. At another time, in a town so small that it had only one church, Billy Young took Lester and Irma to a service where they were obliged to sit on a segregated bench at the back, listening to the preacher railing against the 'black sin' which would condemn the unrepentant to 'the blackest hell of all'. When the moment came to step forward and be 'saved', however, the blacks present were not allowed to join in. With such lessons learned in his childhood, it is hardly surprising that, later in life, Lester appeared withdrawn and suspicious in the presence of white strangers.

From the winter of 1926–7, matters improved considerably. Instead of spending the winter months touring the southern TOBA circuit in Georgia, Alabama or Florida, the family settled for half the year in Minneapolis. Even the notorious Minnesota winter, with temperatures regularly as low as minus 18 degrees Celsius, could not detract from the relief of living in an unsegregated northern city. For one thing, they could stay in one place and get to know people. Billy had rented a big house for the extended family, replete with the luxuries of plumbing and electricity, and even employed a maid to help run it. (This would have given him a measure of quiet satisfaction. One of his oft-repeated mantras was: 'My sons will never be porters; my daughter will never be anyone's maid'.)

Another benefit came in the form of regular schooling. Billy himself had undertaken to give the children lessons while on the road, but he could not really devote sufficient time to the job. They had sporadically attended school during winter sojourns at TOBA theatres, but the elementary education provided for black children in Alabama or Georgia was scarcely worthy of the name, and no one seemed to care whether they turned up or not. The authorities in Minneapolis took a very different attitude. All children of school age, regardless of race, creed or anything else, would attend school regularly, and that was that. Lester was seventeen by this time, and so received little benefit from this new opportunity, and it was the same for Irma, who was fourteen, the age at which compulsory schooling normally finished. Only Lee, ten, received any systematic grounding in basic literacy and numeracy, and it seems to have paid off handsomely, in terms of his social confidence as much as anything. Lester did not grow up entirely illiterate, but he was always ill at ease with the written word, and the same seems to have been true of Irma. Lester's handwriting was quite childish-looking, and when, in later life, he was touring abroad as a famous soloist, he would avoid filling out hotel registration forms, landing cards and similar documents, silently handing them instead to the tour manager and drifting absent-mindedly away.

The more settled existence in Minneapolis was made possible by a change in the type of work available. In large conurbations, such as the twin cities of Minneapolis and St Paul, the modern craze for public dancing was well established. The earthy gusto of the travelling shows, with their slapstick comedy, bawdy repartee and hearty, sing-along tunes, was passing out of fashion. In their place came glossier music, played by bigger bands for dancing crowds. To cater for this new demand, Billy Young enlarged his band to eleven players, but retained the name of the New Orleans Strutters. According to Leonard Phillips, who played trumpet in it, the band now consisted of two trumpets, two trombones, three saxophones, piano, banjo, tuba and drums.[12] Billy Young himself, Phillips recalled, normally played the tuba part, although the one extant photograph of the New Orleans Strutters dating from this time shows him conducting the band while someone else plays the tuba.

No recordings exist of the New Orleans Strutters, but this is a typical dance band line-up of the mid-to-late 1920s, so we can make a fair guess at how they sounded by listening to recordings of contemporary black bands, such as Charlie Johnson's Paradise Orchestra or Andy Preer and his Cotton Club Orchestra. This was the period which saw the birth of the American dance band, whose format of brass, saxophones and rhythm instruments, organized in sections, set a pattern that would be universally adhered to for the next half century and is still widely used today. The brass and saxophone sections take the leading and backing roles by turns, interspersed with instrumental solos and full-band passages. The rhythm section, at this early stage consisting of piano, banjo, tuba (or sousaphone) and drums, provides the harmonic framework and lays down the beat. This simple but immensely flexible set-up has been described as the first entirely new orchestral format in Western music since the emergence of the symphony orchestra in the mid-eighteenth century. Its two most radical innovations were the rhythm section, introduced via marching bands and military music, and the saxophone. Since this is the medium through which Lester Young's genius was to manifest itself, a brief excursion on the subject of the saxophone and its history seems appropriate at this point.

Invented in about 1840 by the Belgian instrument maker Adolphe Sax, the saxophone is a woodwind instrument made of brass. The sound is generated by a single reed resonating on a clarinet-style mouthpiece. Notes are articulated by the raising and lowering of pads covering holes in the elongated brass cone which forms the body of the instrument. Saxophones come in a range, or 'family', of sizes and pitches, from the tiny sopranino to the gargantuan contrabass, but the vast majority fall within the range from soprano to baritone, with the alto and tenor being the most favoured of all. The instrument was originally intended for use in military music, and became a standard feature in the regimental bands of France and some other western European countries by the mid-nineteenth century. It arrived in the United States by way of the popular 'wind bands' of the 1880s, the most celebrated being that of John Philip Sousa, the 'March King'. American instrument manufacturers began mass-producing saxophones, along with other wind instruments, in response to demand from high-school, college, military and town bands, and they quickly came within the reach of all through the brisk turnover of the second-hand trade. At the same time, the saxophone discovered a role on the vaudeville stage. Apart from musical notes, the instrument was found to be capable of producing a number of novelty effects – the neighing of a horse and various farmyard noises, a curious popping sound, like the drawing of a cork (known as 'slap tonguing'), laughter, sobbing, and so on. Groups of saxophonic entertainers, deploying several varieties of the instrument and using these tricks, became quite popular. The Young family band's show included one such act, in which the teenage Lester took part.

It was on such foundations that the American dance orchestra was built, and jazz was a form of popular dance music. In the mid-1920s, the saxophone found itself suddenly fashionable, an icon of the Jazz Age, in exactly the same way as the guitar was to find itself suddenly fashionable in the early 1960s, as an icon of the Rock Age. 'All night long the saxophones wailed the Beale Street Blues', wrote F. Scott Fitzgerald in *The Great Gatsby*, and the wailing or moaning of saxophones often turns up in writing of the period. It symbolized a whole package of notions that went to make up the popular zeitgeist – the Lost Generation, doomed youth, hedonism, an attraction to the primitive and elemental. The speed with which this happened was remarkable, bearing in mind the rudimentary state of the mass media. The first jazz bands to make records contained no saxophones at all, yet within a few years the very idea of a hot jazz band without at least one saxophone was quite unthinkable. Take the case of the New Orleans pioneer King Oliver. His first, and today his most admired, recordings were made with his eight-piece Creole Jazz Band, its melody instruments being two cornets, clarinet and trombone. That was in 1923. Three years later he was leading the ten-piece Dixie Syncopators – two trumpets, trombone and three saxophones.

So, in restyling his New Orleans Strutters as an eleven-piece dance orchestra in 1927, Billy Young was conforming exactly to the prevailing trend. In Minneapolis, the band played regularly at the South Side Ballroom and at two big hotels, the Radisson and the St Paul. It also undertook a brief tour in North and South Dakota. It was during a stopover in Bismarck, North Dakota, that Lester heard a record by Frankie Trumbauer, the saxophonist who was to be his first and only admitted influence. The record belonged to Eddie Barefield, a musician who was lodging in the same rooming house.

> I heard a knock on the door and he opened the door. 'I'm Lester Young. Who's that playing saxophone?' I said, 'Frankie Trumbauer.' He said, 'Do you mind if I listen?' So he came in and we met.[13]

Lester and Eddie Barefield became close friends and spent hours together, listening to records and learning from them. They were both born in the same year, 1909, and the first substantial body of recorded music came into existence during their teenage years. They were therefore part of the first generation in human history able to listen to music without having to be physically present while it was being played, and thus able to study music closely by purely aural means. The implications of this are too vast to go into here, but they account, among other things, for the worldwide spread of jazz in the twentieth century. Had recordings not existed, the chances of Lester Young experiencing the playing of Frankie Trumbauer would have been slim, to say the least.

In fact, Lester's ear was first beguiled by two players, both white: Trumbauer and Jimmy Dorsey.

Frankie Trumbauer and Jimmy Dorsey were battling for honours in those days, and I finally found out that I liked Frankie Trumbauer. Trumbauer was my idol. When I started to play I used to buy all his records. I imagine I can still play all those solos off the record. He played the c-melody saxophone. I tried to get the sound of a c-melody on a tenor. That's why I don't sound like other people. Trumbauer always told a little story, and I liked the way he slurred his notes. He'd play the melody first and then after that he'd play around the melody.[14]

[Trumbauer], that was my man... Did you ever hear him play 'Singing The Blues'? That tricked me right there. That's where I went.[15]

So who was Frankie Trumbauer, and what was it about his playing that attracted the youthful Lester? Orie Frank Trumbauer, often known by the nickname 'Tram', was born on 30 May 1901 at Carbondale, Illinois. As a young man he was very handsome and is reputed once to have been offered the job of stand-in for Rudolph Valentino. His main instrument was the c-melody saxophone, a variety now extinct, pitched higher than the tenor but lower than the alto. On record his sound has a fragile, keening quality, almost devoid of vibrato, and his articulation is very precise. The recording of 'Singing The Blues' mentioned by Lester was made in 1927, and would have been brand new when he heard it for the first time in Eddie Barefield's room. Trumbauer plays the opening solo with a typically light touch, adding a few whimsical asides, before handing over to Bix Beiderbecke's cornet solo. From what we know of Lester's gentle, unassertive nature, it is easy to understand what it was about Trumbauer's playing that appealed to him. He would also have been attracted by the pinpoint accuracy of the technique. The saxophone may have been all the rage in 1927, but it was not, on the whole, a well-played instrument. Unlike the trumpet or the piano, it had no tradition of great performers to act as role models. The 'wailing' saxophone of *The Great Gatsby* was more a kind of low, mooing noise, interspersed with the occasional rubbery belch. It cannot have been an encouraging instrument for a young man to find himself struggling with. Amidst all the surrounding hooting and gargling, Trumbauer's precision and restraint must have been irresistible.

We have no way of knowing which of Trumbauer's records, apart from 'Singing The Blues', Lester listened to. No doubt the ones featuring Bix Beiderbecke, such as 'For No Reason At All In C' and 'Wringin' And Twistin'', figured among them, together with those on which the c-melody saxophone plays a leading role, including 'The Baltimore' and 'There's A Cradle In Caroline'. Trumbauer's influence is clearly audible in Lester's own early recordings – the little scooping inflexions, the sudden rip up to an isolated high note and the curiously floating quality in the tone.

Trumbauer himself later gave up the music profession to work in aeronautics. He served as a test pilot in World War II and died in 1956. His widow, Mitzy, recalled a number of strange semi-encounters that took place between him and Lester in the late 1930s:

> Tram was playing with Paul Whiteman and sometimes after he'd finished for the evening we'd go up to Harlem to hear Count Basie and Lester Young... I think sometimes Lester would recognise him, because he'd look over and give a funny little movement of his head, and Tram would smile and nod back. But I don't think they ever spoke. Lester seemed very shy and Frank was part Indian and never used two words where one would do, but they seemed to understand and respect each other.[16]

According to Leonard Phillips, Lester's other favourites included Bix Beiderbecke and Benny Goodman, who was almost exactly Lester's age and had just begun his recording career as a member of Ben Pollack's orchestra. They are both entirely plausible as choices, Beiderbecke for his sunny lyricism and Goodman for his sparkling clarinet technique. He also listened closely to the showy, light-classical virtuoso Rudy Wiedoft. The fact that most of Lester's early favourites were white musicians has proved inconvenient to those tidy-minded theorists who take the view that black jazz musicians influence white ones, never vice versa. As we shall see, his habit of infuriating such people by failing to stick to the approved line was one of his many endearing qualities.

Lester's method of studying was typically idiosyncratic and relied entirely on his exceptional ear and memory. He could walk into a record store, listen to a piece once and not only play it through later but harmonize it by dictation. Even this was not done in a straightforward way. It was easier to play the notes than name them, so his dictation proceeded by a series of short bursts – 'You play this' (blows a short phrase), 'And you play this' (another phrase). 'Now both play together'. Then on to the next phrase, and so on.

In late 1927, one of those periodic outbreaks of gangster violence which were routine occurrences during Prohibition was followed, in Minneapolis, by an equally routine outbreak of moral panic. As a result, hotels and ballrooms found themselves under heavy surveillance and a midnight curfew. This probably caused little inconvenience to the criminal fraternity, but it severely restricted work opportunities for bands. Billy Young decided that it was time to move on and began setting up a tour which would take them south, through Texas and New Mexico and eventually to Arizona. Having settled into the relatively unprejudiced atmosphere of Minneapolis, Lester was reluctant to leave. He tried to talk his father out of the idea: 'I told him how it would be down there, and that we could have some fine jobs back through Nebraska, Kansas and Iowa, but he didn't have eyes for that. He was set to go.'[17]

The tour began, with Lester still vainly lobbying for a change of plan. It was when they reached Salina, Kansas, that he gave up the attempt, announced that he was not prepared to endure the indignities of a southern tour and resigned. He was eighteen years old and perfectly entitled to do so, but it must have taken courage to face the wrath of an outraged of Billy Young. The old man made him leave his instruments behind when he left, on the grounds that they were the band's, not Lester's own. The band, minus Lester, moved on, but before long two more mutineers, Leonard Phillips and trombonist Pete Jones, defected. 'We didn't want to go back to no damn carnival', Phillips explained later. 'You don't get no prestige playing on a carnival!'[18] They jumped ship in Wichita and caught a bus back to Salina, where they found Lester enjoying a game of pool at a local musicians' hangout. He greeted them joyfully. He had already found himself a temporary gig, playing at the Wiggly Café on a borrowed alto saxophone, and he had some good news for them all. 'There's a guy here got a band he wants to enlarge to a ten-piece!', he announced.[19] It seemed that they had fallen on their feet.

2 the territory

The guy in question was a pianist named Art Bronson, and the six-piece band he was seeking to enlarge was known as the Bostonians. Since it came originally from Denver, Colorado, was now based in Salina, Kansas, and had no known connection with Boston or New England, the reason for its name remains a mystery.

The Bostonians was one of the species known as 'territory bands', which flourished particularly in the south- and mid-west during the 1920s and early 1930s. A brief glance at a map of the United States will reveal one simple fact as you read from east to west, namely that the states become larger and the main centres of population further apart. On the ground, this pattern manifests itself in immense vistas of farmland and prairie, crossed by endless straight roads, with mountains to the north and west. Scattered throughout are smaller towns, often at points where roads or railroad lines meet, with more remote communities beyond. It was these towns and settlements which constituted the 'territory'. They were too small and dispersed to support much of an entertainment structure of their own, but their inhabitants wanted to enjoy themselves in their limited leisure time and increasingly had the means to afford it. The post-war craze for public dancing attracted young people every-where, while mass-produced automobiles and improved roads enabled travelling bands to cater to the demand.

The Bostonians covered the area which Lester had tried vainly to per-suade his father to stick to – Kansas, Nebraska and the Dakotas – riding in a Buick station wagon, followed by a truck carrying the instruments. The itinerary took in the Indian reservations in South Dakota where, according to Leonard Phillips, 'the Indians were into the blues'.[1] The ten-piece band attracted crowds of up to 3,000, which leads one to wonder how they managed to make themselves heard in those days before microphones and public address systems.

The alto saxophone was still Lester's principal instrument, but the chance soon came for him to change to the tenor. Bronson's tenor player was something of a dilettante, according to Lester. He came from a fairly well-off background and had never needed to rely on music for a living.

His casual approach to the serious business of work infuriated those members of the band, Lester included, who had been raised in the school of hard knocks.

> We'd all be ready. We'd be waiting for ninety years to get us to work, you know. And he said: 'Wait for me until I get my shirt on, and get my tie on', and all that shit, and everybody'll be waiting, disgusted. So I told the boss man – his name was Art Bronson – I said: 'Listen, why should we go through all this shit?' I said, 'You buy me a tenor saxophone and I'll play the motherfucker and we'll be straight then.' And he went to the music store, got me a tenor sax and we split. As soon as I got my mouth round it, I knew it was for me. That alto was a little high for me.[2]

It was a Conn Pan-American tenor, a model not much favoured by professional players, and old, to boot. 'When I saw the beat-up old tenor he bought, though, I almost changed my mind... But I played it, and I liked it, what's more.'[3] Although he still occasionally played alto, and even baritone, in these early days, the tenor became his true instrument from this point on.

Figure 3. 1928. Salina, Kansas. The saxophone section of Art Bronson's Bostonians (l to r): Lester, Odie Cromwell, Sam Allen. (Frank Driggs collection)

Keeping track of Lester Young's comings and goings during this period is difficult, especially when it comes to pinning down dates and the exact sequence of events. Even those diligent scholars Frank Büchmann-Møller and Prof. Douglas Henry Daniels come up with slightly differing accounts. It seems, however, that Lester stayed with Bronson until the beginning of 1929, and then returned to his family, which had settled for a while in Albuquerque, New Mexico. In addition to running the band, Billy and Sarah Young had opened their own music shop, and Billy had also acquired an interest in *The Trend*, a local paper for the black community, published fortnightly.

Settling back into the family band's routine, Lester made the acquaintance of a young man of his own age, formerly a pianist, who was working hard at mastering the tenor saxophone. This was Ben Webster, himself destined to become one of the great jazz voices of the instrument. Billy Young taught him to read music and Lester would sit and practise with him every day. Always a big man, Ben at that age was also superbly fit and a very strong swimmer. These attributes turned out to be more than useful during the summer of 1929. When the young people were swimming in the Rio Grande, Lester got into difficulties; Ben dived in and dragged him ashore, only to find Lee stuck in a sand-hole. 'I was only a little boy, about ten or eleven', Lee recalled (in fact, he was twelve). 'He just picked me up under one arm and carried me home.'

All in all, his stay in Albuquerque proved an eventful one for Lester. It was here that he met and married Beatrice Tolliver, his first wife, on 23 February 1930. He gave 27 August 1908, not 1909, as his date of birth, thereby advancing his age to twenty-one. This may indicate that either he had not sought his father's permission, or had asked and been refused. In view of Billy Young's autocratic style, it was probably the former. In any case, the deed was done. Beatrice, originally from Oklahoma, was aged eighteen and worked as a maid in the home of an Albuquerque doctor. The newlyweds briefly set up home in rented rooms and then appear to have moved to Minneapolis, which Lester had come to regard as his home town. The tale of Lester's marriages and liaisons is a tangled one, and a particularly deep mystery surrounds his personal life in Minneapolis at this time. He seems to have taken up with a white woman called Bess Cooper, by whom he had a daughter, named Beverly. No documents survive, but an interview with Beverly, then aged fifty-four, was featured in the *Minneapolis Star & Tribune* of 25 August 1985. In it, she says that her mother, Bess, died soon after giving birth to her and that she had been brought up by foster parents. She recalls her father with great affection, and claims that he kept in touch with her until the end of his life, visited her whenever he could, bought her a piano, and even took her on tour with him occasionally. What became of Beatrice while this drama was unfolding no one seems to know. Possibly she remained in Albuquerque for a while and joined Lester in Minneapolis later. Whatever the case, they appear to have been together throughout the early 1930s.

Upon arriving back in Minneapolis, Lester had a reunion with Eddie Barefield, and the pair of them teamed up briefly to work as a saxophone duo. Exactly how they managed, without any form of rhythm accompaniment, it is impossible to say, but Barefield insisted that they had played for school dances and the like.[4] Soon, however, Lester accepted an offer to join the Blue Devils, a band whose name has become part of the creation-myth of jazz. Through it passed not only Lester Young, but Count Basie, Hot Lips Page and Buster Smith, who was to be Charlie Parker's mentor. The band's mythical status derives from the fact that it recorded only once, and the resulting two pieces are widely regarded as unrepresentative. Basie, in his memoirs, claims that hearing the Blue Devils for the first time was a transforming moment in his life, 'the greatest thing I ever heard'. First formed in the early 1920s and led by Walter Page, who played tuba, double bass and occasionally baritone saxophone, the Blue Devils was a co-operative or 'commonwealth' band, in which each member held an equal stake. Despite its great reputation among territory bands, it made nobody rich, and its members were constantly being poached away by rivals, whose recruiting methods involved 'offers, sales-talk, raids and cajolery – all part of the in-fighting of the dance band business'.[5]

This was to be the first of Lester's spells with the Blue Devils. It proved to be a short one and was passed at the Ritz Ballroom in Oklahoma City. At the end of that engagement the band was due to move on to Little Rock, Arkansas, a prospect which he would not have relished. He returned instead to Minneapolis and signed on for another tour with Art Bronson. Throughout this period, Lester's home was in Minneapolis. It was the place he returned to at the end of a tour or residency and, as far as we know, Beatrice was there waiting for him. Also, as far as we know, Beverly was growing up with her foster parents in the same city. He had not been settled in one place as long as this since the age of ten, and it seems to have suited him because he took a series of jobs with local bands, beginning with his old pal Eddie Barefield at the Nest Club, followed by Eugene Schuck's Cotton Club Orchestra, the orchestras of Frank Hines and Paul Cepha, and Gene Coy and his Happy Black Aces. Then, around the middle of 1932, it was back to the Blue Devils.

Walter Page had now left, after handing over the leadership to vocalist Ernest Williams. At first, Lester refused to budge from Minneapolis, but was finally persuaded when arrangements were made for Beatrice to accompany him. The couple teamed up with trumpeter Leroy 'Snake' White, his wife and infant son, and they all shared accommodation on the road. They also travelled in style in a brand new Ford station wagon. There was one fatal flaw in the Blue Devils' 'commonwealth' system, and that was its lack of a cash reserve. The band paid its way and met its expenses, and the remaining money was scrupulously divided into thirteen equal shares, but there was no cushion to keep the thing going if they experienced even a minor blockage in cash flow. At a settled residency in known territory, such as the Ritz Ballroom, Oklahoma City, there was little danger of this, but a tour through Kentucky and West Virginia, well off their usual track and in the middle of the Depression, brought disaster. Thin audiences, shady promoters, late payments, bills unmet – the whole thing quickly unravelled, and in May 1933, in Newport News, Virginia, their instruments were impounded.

'We never did make any money,' Buster Smith recalled, 'and when we got thrown out of our hotel everybody got disgusted. One of the fellows wrote home for the train fare, and the rest of us left by freight.'[6]

Lester remembered the disconsolate little group of men hanging around at the edge of a freight yard. (Presumably, family members had not joined this ill-fated tour.)

> There we were, sitting around with these hoboes, and they showed us how to grab a train. We made it, with bruises. We got to Cincinnati, no loot, no horns, all ragged and dirty, and we were trying to make it to St Louis or Kansas City. I found a man who had an alto and loaned it out for gigs, so I managed to play a couple of dates. Finally, we all had a meeting, and we decided it was 'every tub' – every man for himself.[7]

And so ended the career of the revered Blue Devils.

Lester finally made it to Kansas City. No sooner had he arrived than he spied the familiar face of Pete Jones, who had played trombone in the Young family band. 'Hey man! I'm in bad shape. I'm broke, I ain't got no money, ain't got no clothes, ain't got nothing! If you got a job for me, I'm gonna take it. I ain't working... I hoboed all the way back from Virginia!'[8] And, as luck would have it, Pete Jones did have a job. He was now a member of King Oliver's touring band, and was in town with Oliver on a scouting expedition for a new tenor saxophonist. Lester was recruited on the spot, and when Oliver and Jones took him to meet the band, he found another old friend, Leonard Phillips, ensconced in the trumpet section. In fact, Oliver had recently hijacked the entire Art Bronson band, by offering them more money and the prestige of playing for a star leader. 'Man!' exclaimed Phillips, 'We got a tenor player now!'[9]

King Oliver was in his declining years. One of the great figures of the New Orleans migration in the first decades of the century, he had managed to hang on through the transition to the dance band era by making a speciality of 'preaching' or 'talking' trumpet. His ability to produce vocal effects through the use of mutes was quite uncanny. His recorded solos on 'Dippermouth Blues' (1923) and 'Sugar Blues' (1931), for example, are so remarkable that everyone who has subsequently played these pieces has repeated them virtually note-for-note, complete with attempts to reproduce Oliver's unearthly, crying inflexions. But the recording session which produced 'Sugar Blues' turned out to be his next-to-last. His contract with the Brunswick label was not renewed and he was forced to rely on touring for an income. Apart from being a bad time economically, the early 1930s saw the beginnings of a shift in public taste away from his style of jazz. In addition, Oliver was suffering from the gum disease pyorrhoea, which made playing increasingly difficult, especially for a player who depended on his peculiar kind of virtuosity.

Lester remembered Oliver with affection:

> He had a very nice band and I worked regularly with him...around Kansas and Missouri mostly. He had three brass, three reeds and four rhythms. He was playing well. He was old then and didn't play all night [Oliver was actually aged forty-eight], but his tone was full when he played. He was the star of the show and played one or two songs each set... He could play some nice blues. He was a very nice fellow, a gay old fellow. He was crazy about all the boys and it wasn't a drag playing for him at all.[10]

For six months, in the latter part of 1933, Lester toured around Missouri, Kansas and Oklahoma as a member of King Oliver's band. He was now twenty-four years old and much of the previous six years had been spent travelling around the mid- and south-western states. The world at large may not have heard of him, but there cannot have been many musicians who did not know him, at least by reputation. The novelist Ralph Ellison, born and brought up in Oklahoma City, encountered him there at a jam session in Haille Richardson's shoeshine parlour:

> I first heard Lester Young jamming in a shine chair, his head thrown back, his feet working the footrests, as he played with and against Lem Johnson, Ben Webster and members of the old Blue Devils orchestra... A tall, intense young musician, with his heavy white sweater, blue stock-

ing cap and up-and-out thrust silver saxophone, he left absolutely no reed player and few young players of any instrument unstirred by the wild, excitingly original flights of his imagination. Lester Young, with his battered horn, upset the entire Negro section of the town.[11]

The word quickly got about that there was a shy, dreamy young man drifting around among the territory bands whose style and sound on the tenor were quite unlike anyone else's, and who was scaring all the other saxophone players to death. Another saxophonist, Buddy Tate, remembered meeting Lester when the family band had passed through his home town of Sherman, Texas. They had both been teenagers at the time, but Tate realized that this must now be the man all the fuss was about, and was eager to hear for himself. The chance came in Tulsa, Oklahoma.

> Down in the lobby of the hotel where we were staying they had a piano, and musicians used to come in and jam. And someone says, 'Lester's upstairs!'. So I thought I'd go wake him up, make him play some! I went up to his room. He was lying there with corn pads on his toes, and I woke him up, and he says, 'Oh, really! Well wait. Can you wait till I get my clothes on?' He just loved to play. And he just jumped into his clothes right quick and came downstairs and started to blowing. Man! I shall always remember the sounds that came out of that horn!'[12]

According to Buddy Tate, all the other players simply sat there in stunned silence, until Lester said, 'Look, I didn't come down here to give a concert!' He loved the give-and-take of a jam session, where he could take turns with other players, test himself and swap musical ideas. A jam session was a mixture of social event, competitive examination and educational experience, and it was strictly for insiders. There was no audience; everyone present, even the occasional non-player, was a participant. An audience can be impressed by tricks, or dazzled by fame or seduced by charm, but these counted for nothing at a jam session. The only thing that mattered was what you could do and how well you could do it. Sometimes, simply being allowed to take part was enough to get a player onto the bottom rung of the professional ladder. If he made a decent showing in tough company, his stock went up. If not, he was cast back into outer darkness, 'back to the woodshed', to practise and maybe try again. Even the great Charlie Parker was to suffer this ignominious fate on his first attempt.

The jam-session tradition was particularly strong in the south- and mid-west. Musicians who were forever on the move over great distances relished the chance to meet others, to exchange gossip and shop-talk and above all to play together. Out of these gatherings grew the musical language in which they were conducted, an entire vocabulary of melodies, chord structures, turns of phrase and tones of voice. One notable characteristic of this language was its use of a device known as the riff. A riff is a phrase, usually two or four bars in length, which can be repeated over and over, with small alterations to accommodate any harmonic changes. Riffs can serve as themes for improvisation, as accompaniment to a soloist, or superimposed one on another as a form of instant orchestration. Riffs were to become a hugely important ingredient in jazz over the coming years.

The territory happened to coincide with that region of the United States in which the folk tradition of the blues was strongest, a great triangle with its base points in Texas to the west and Georgia to the east, and its apex around Kansas City. Within this triangle the blues in all its many varieties flourished, and its accents flavoured every note that these musicians played. The blues evolved originally as a folk idiom, a discursive vocal music concerned with expressing feelings and telling stories. As such, it was not contained within a strict, metric form. When blues singers accompanied themselves on instruments, the accompaniment usually followed the vocal line. In this, the blues was quite distinct from the popular music of the north-eastern states, such as the one-step, the vaudeville song or ragtime, all of which followed the norms of formal European music. Ragtime was set within a framework of regular beats, divided into bars denoted by time-signatures, and its phrasing, melody and harmony fitted into the same symmetrical pattern. The syncopation, or 'ragged time', which gave ragtime its name, achieved its spicy effect by creating a mild disturbance of this symmetry. In south-western jazz, these two traditions met – the fluid, singing line of the blues and the insistent, forward-moving regularity of ragtime and its successors – and from the pull of one against the other emerged the mysterious and magical quality known as 'swing', which has no exact counterpart in any other form of music on earth.[13]

Virtually the whole of Lester Young's life had been passed in blues country, with the blues as the musical *lingua franca*. It was no accident, therefore, that he talked about playing music as 'telling your story', or that his own playing was at first to prove so strange to eastern ears, when they finally got to hear it.

Lester quit King Oliver's band in November 1933, probably because a tour of the Deep South was in the offing, and returned to Kansas City, which he had now decided to make his base. It was a lively town. Prohibition had recently been repealed but no one in Kansas City seemed to notice, because no one had paid any attention to it in the first place.

For the previous decade-and-a-half the city had been run by a gang-ster-politician named Tom Pendergast and his sidekick, Johnny Lazia. The place had more dives, brothels, gin-mills, dancehalls, cabarets and gambling dens per head of population than anywhere else in the United States. In the words of Maurice Milligan, the District Attorney who finally brought down the Pendergast empire: 'With the possible exception of such renowned centres as Singapore and Port Said, Kansas City probably has the greatest sin industry in the world.'[14] Situated at the confluence of two major rivers and the junction of seven major railroad lines, it was the business centre of the west. And what could be more pleasant after a day's hard dealing than a little fun and games? 'When the underworld flocks to...Kansas City, it has to be entertained on a wild and lavish scale. It demands music, women and gambling tables, and while engaged in the pursuit of high life it wants protection from snoopers, reformers and policemen who may be a bit overzealous in upholding the law.'[15] The system took good care of that, too. In 1933, the year Lester Young took up residence, ten per cent of the city's police force possessed known criminal records.

Deplorable though it may be, and offensive to virtuous opinion, it is an undeniable fact that jazz music has generally flourished under these conditions. Such was certainly the case in Kansas City, as even the reforming District Attorney was forced to admit:

> In Kansas City a whole new school of jazz music was born. Bennie Moten, Count Basie, Walter 'Hot Lips' Page [sic]; Andy Kirk and others kept the Reno Club and other hot spots jumping with rhythm. I am no authority on jazz, and must take the word of others about this phase of Kansas City's cultural renaissance. The only point I would like to make is that all this flourished during the Pendergast era and because of it.[16]

Just as Kansas City (or 'Kaycee') ignored the strictures of prohibition, so it escaped the worst effects of the depression. With its prodigious nightlife and non-stop jam sessions, there was certainly no lack of work or stimulus for musicians. The hours were long and the pay terrible, but standards were ferociously high. Lester found a temporary place in Clarence Love's band at the El Torreon Ballroom and, a few weeks later, joined the Bennie Moten orchestra for its opening at the Club Harlem. Although it had recently suffered a few setbacks, Moten's was the most prestigious black band in the south-west and it occupies a pivotal posi-tion in the history and evolution of the American jazz orchestra. From obscure beginnings in the early 1920s, it had grown in size and stature, partly by swallowing its competitors. It was to Moten that Walter Page had defected when the difficulty of leading the Blue Devils became too much for him. Others followed until, by 1932, Moten's band had become virtually the Blue Devils in exile. It had now formed an alliance with another major rival, the singer, entertainer and former bandleader George E. Lee.

Bennie Moten, a Kansas City native, was originally a pianist, although in latter days he confined himself to waving an elegant, if superfluous, baton. He was a shrewd operator, with an eye for economic micro-climates. He knew, for example, the paydays of local industries and put on his own dance promotions to coincide with them.[17] He was in good standing with Pendergast and his minions but had a personal reputation among musicians for honesty and fair dealing. Unlike other south-western bands, Bennie Moten's Kansas City Orchestra managed to record quite regularly through the late 1920s and early 1930s, and by listening to its records in chronological order it is possible to trace the changes, especially rhythmic changes, which took place in jazz over those years. To take just two of the best-known examples: 'South' (recorded September 1928) has all the hallmarks of 1920s dance music, although it is too accomplished to be a typical product of its time. It is carried on a two-beat rhythm, in which the first and third beats of each bar are emphasized. This is played by a rhythm section consisting of piano, banjo, tuba (or sousaphone) and drums. The tuba plods along doughtily, the banjo clanks, the drums roll and clatter. It's all quite laborious, although the effect in this case is jaunty and cheerful. 'Moten Swing', on the other hand (recorded December 1932), has four even beats to the bar. Instead of bumping along, it drives smoothly and the whole thing is much lighter in texture. The tuba has been replaced by a double bass, the banjo has given way to a guitar, the drummer confines himself to creating a propul-sive beat. To put it in a nutshell, 'South' is in the old style that King Oliver was still playing, whereas in the aptly-named 'Moten Swing' we find a harbinger of the coming age.

If Lester Young had been with Moten at the end of 1932, instead of away with the Blue Devils in Oklahoma, his recording career might have commenced earlier and we should know what he really sounded like in those days. As it is, the eight-bar tenor saxophone solo on 'Moten Swing' is played by his erstwhile practice partner (and saviour from a watery grave), Ben Webster. The alto saxophonist is Lester's old friend Eddie Barefield, and the pianist, soon destined to play an important role in Lester's life, is one Bill Basie. Shortly before Lester's arrival, some kind of palace revolution had occurred in the Moten ranks, resulting in the departure of Basie and several others to form their own band under

Basie's leadership. Exactly when and how Bill Basie was elevated to the peerage has never been properly established, but it was as Count Basie that he was ensconced as bandleader at the Cherry Blossom on Vine Street, Kansas City. His tenor saxophonist was Herschel Evans, and at some point in February 1934 Herschel and Lester swapped jobs.

Like every other tenor saxophone player in the world, with the apparently sole exception of Lester Young, Herschel Evans lived in awe of Coleman Hawkins. Hawkins was the man who had, to all intents and purposes, invented the tenor saxophone as a jazz instrument. His beefy sound and urgent, snapping phrases set the standard by which all other players were judged. They treated him with something of the awed respect which classical cellists accorded Pablo Casals. There was majesty in Hawkins's playing, informed by a mind and an ear so comprehensive that the idea of anyone ever challenging him seemed laughable. He steamed imperiously ahead, like a liner through a heavy swell, his great voice booming out over the waves as a warning to others. Naturally, Lester knew all about Coleman Hawkins. He would have heard him on record, and listened to the gushing admiration of other tenor players. Now it seemed he would have a chance to hear him in person. Fletcher Henderson's celebrated orchestra, of which Hawkins was the undoubted star, was coming to play a show in Kansas City.

'I'd always heard so much about Hawk,' Lester recalled. 'I ran over to dig him between sets. I hadn't any loot so I stayed outside listening... Herschel was out there, too.'[18] But Hawkins had failed to show up.

> I ran a million miles to hear Coleman Hawkins play and he wasn't there. So Fletcher Henderson ran out saying, "Don't you have no tenor players here in Kansas City? Can any of you play?"... Herschel was out there, you dig, but he couldn't read. So they say, "Red!" (they called me Red then) "Red, go and blow this goddam saxophone!" And I'm coming to see Coleman Hawkins, they told me how great he was!... So they showed me in and I get up and grabbed his saxophone and played the mother-fucker and read the music and read his clarinet parts and everything. Now I got to run back to my job where there's thirteen people in it. Run ten blocks to get to 'em!'[19]

There is nothing mythical about this story. Not only did Lester tell it in detail to several interviewers at different times, there were other people present who remembered exactly the same series of events, including the bit about Herschel being scared because his reading wasn't up to it. However you look at it, it was an awesome feat on Lester's part. Setting aside the difficulty of playing on a strange instrument (and, more to the point, a strange mouthpiece), there is the fact that Henderson's arrangements were tricky affairs, beset with key-changes and busy, close harmony passages for the saxophones. Then there's the matter of improvised solos. It was not the practice, in 1934, to write chord symbols on a band part as a harmonic guide for the soloist, and even if they had been there they would not have been of any use to Lester because, as he once admitted, he never really got the hang of chord symbols anyway. So, for solos he had to depend entirely on his phenomenal ear. And, on top of all that, there's the sheer stress of being pitched into the middle of a famous band, in place of the star turn, with no rehearsal, in front of an audience, and with Herschel Evans and half the tenor players in Kansas City listening outside. Fletcher Henderson was mightily impressed, as indeed he should have been.

Lester got to hear Hawkins soon afterwards – not only hear him but play with him at a jam session, and this time a certain mythic aura does surround the tale. Henderson's band was in town again and Hawkins (whose nickname, for some unaccountable reason, was 'Bean') was persuaded to take part in an after-hours jam session at the Cherry Blossom. The best-known account of what happened there is the one given by Mary Lou Williams, pianist at the time with Andy Kirk's Clouds of Joy:

> The word went round that Hawkins was in the Cherry Blossom, and within about half an hour there were Lester Young, Ben Webster, Herschel Evans, Herman Walder, and one or two unknown tenors piling into the club to blow. Bean didn't know the Kaycee men were so terrific, and he couldn't get himself together although he played all the morning. I happened to be nodding that night, and at around four a.m. I awoke to hear someone pecking on my screen. I opened the window on Ben Webster. He was saying, 'Get up, pussycat! We're jammin' and all the pianists are tired out now. Hawkins has got his shirt off and is still blowing. You got to come down!
>
> 'Sure enough, when we got there, Hawkins was in his singlet, taking turns with the Kaycee men. It seems he had run into something he didn't expect. Lester's style was light and, as I said, it took him maybe five choruses to warm up. But then he would really blow; then you couldn't handle him on a cutting session. That was how Hawkins got hung up. The Henderson band was playing in St Louis that evening, and Bean knew he ought to be on his way. But he kept trying to blow something to beat Ben and Herschel and Lester. When at last he gave up, he got straight in his car and drove to St Louis. I heard he'd just bought a new Cadillac and that he burnt it out trying to make the job on time.
>
> 'Yes, Hawkins was king until he met those crazy Kansas City tenor men!'[20]

The story of the routing of Hawkins is one of the great myths of jazz, taking 'myth' in the sense of 'a tale concerning heroes, handed down from antiquity'. If it isn't literally true in every detail – the singlet, the Cadillac, the epic length of the session – it represents in emblematic form all that Kaycee stood for.

In March 1934, Basie's ten-piece band left Kansas City for a longish engagement in Little Rock, Arkansas. Lester knew the place well. He'd been there before, with the Blue Devils. He was not particularly ambitious or avid for fame, but neither was he a simpleton. He must by now have formed a pretty clear idea of his own powers and the extent of his own potential. Other musicians held him in awe, especially after the recent Henderson and Hawkins episodes, yet here he was, approaching the age of twenty-five, still playing with obscure bands in dancehalls and nightclubs out in the sticks, still living hand-to-mouth, still not part of the action. He even wrote to a friend in New York, the trumpeter George Dixon, asking him to keep an eye out for openings there.[21]

Coleman Hawkins was also feeling dissatisfied. He had been with Fletcher Henderson since 1924 and was in urgent need of a change. He, too, wrote a letter, to the British bandleader Jack Hylton, saying that he was interested in coming to England if something could be arranged. Hylton replied with a very satisfactory offer and Hawkins duly handed in his notice to Henderson. What happened next depends on who's telling the story. According to George Dixon, he showed Henderson Lester's letter and Henderson phoned Lester in Little Rock. According to Lester, a cable from Henderson arrived out of the blue, with no prompting from him. According to the critic, talent-spotter and recording director John Hammond, Henderson already had Lester in mind.

> He was having a lot of trouble with the band [Hammond recalled]. He didn't have a decent agent. Everything was falling apart. He came to me and said, 'I heard a band out in Kansas City so good that I'd like to fire everybody I've got and hire them.' And I said, 'Well, does it have a good tenor player, because that's what you're looking for?' And he said, 'Absolutely the best, and his name is Lester Young'.[22]

When the call came, however, Lester was scared. He unburdened himself to Buddy Tate: 'He said, "I think I could make it, but I understand the band is full of cliques, and I just don't know how they'll treat me"... I said, go ahead and take it because if you don't like it you can always come back. He said, "Yes, but the part that hurts is to go and be a failure and come back and face your friends".'[23]

The prospect of being cast out, of facing coldness, hostility, rejection, terrified him. The fall from grace when he had been excluded from the family band had, as we know, affected him deeply. Among friends and colleagues who knew and admired him, Lester's personality blossomed and he became the loveable, eccentric genius. In a hostile environment he shrank within himself and became once again a frightened child, snatched from the mother he adored. If Basie had refused to let him go, or even just asked him to stay, his nerve might well have cracked. But Basie made no objection. In fact, he congratulated him and wished him luck.

Lester had been earning $14 a week with Basie; with Henderson, this jumped to $75. Even so, perhaps because he felt lost and nervous in New York, he accepted Henderson's offer to put him up at his own home. His arrival in the band was noted in the entertainment pages of the African-American press. The *Chicago Defender* of 14 April 1934 announced: 'Two new men have joined the Henderson band, Elmer James, bass player, and Lester Young of Kansas City, one of the most celebrated Negro tenor sax players in the music world'. John Hammond, who had not yet heard Lester play, wrote: 'Hawkins's successor is a sensation, I'm told. I haven't heard this redheaded star [but] no less than ten swell Harlemites have told me that he swings more than Hawkins, and has actually "cut" the Master on occasions.'[24]

This kind of attention would have served only to increase his nervousness. At the very first rehearsal it soon became clear that something was wrong. No one could fault Lester's sight-reading or general musicianship, but there just wasn't enough of him. His light, agile tone simply would not fill the space previously occupied by Hawkins. The best way to get some idea of the problem is to listen to the four tunes recorded at Hawkins's last session with Henderson, on 6 March 1934, a month before Lester's arrival.[25] Hawkins takes solos on all four, but it is the overall sound of the reed section that one should focus on. It is an unusual configuration – clarinet, two alto saxophones and one tenor. Theoretically, it should sound unbalanced, with too many highs and not enough lows. But Hawkins's tone is so heavy that it easily acts as a counterweight. Now imagine Hawkins removed and replaced by a tenor voice of about half that weight. The voicing doesn't stick together and the whole thing becomes unstable.

The rumours he had heard were true. The Henderson band was very clannish and clique-ridden, and its members turned on the newcomer. They pointedly ignored him and complained loudly about him to anyone who would listen. They made it quite clear that they had wanted the job to go to Chu Berry, a leading Hawkins disciple. Henderson was not a forceful man and one has the impression that he allowed himself to be bullied by his own band on occasion. At the same time, he was utterly enchanted by Lester's solo playing. John Hammond's first opportunity to hear Lester came in a New York rehearsal room, where he also witnessed Fletcher Henderson's dilemma.

> They couldn't stand him. Buster Bailey [clarinettist] *really* couldn't stand him. Hilton Jefferson [alto saxophonist]...the whole sax section... They said it sounds like another alto, the section doesn't have any body this way. They explained in great detail what was wrong, and Fletcher went along with it... [Then Lester] would get up and play, you know, and I just couldn't believe my ears. I'd never heard anything like this in my life. And I said, 'Fletcher, he's just the best saxophone player I ever heard!' And Fletcher said, 'I know he is, John, but nobody likes him!'[26]

As Henderson fretted and fussed, his wife, Leora, decided to take action. She was a strong-minded woman and something of a power behind the throne. With Lester a virtual captive in her house, she undertook to re-educate him by means of a crash course in Coleman Hawkins. She woke him in the morning to the sound of Hawkins records; she chivvied him around music shops in search of reeds and mouthpieces that would put flesh on his tone; she scolded him brightly, like a ward-sister with a recalcitrant patient. No doubt she meant well, but Lester was mortified. 'I had in mind what I wanted to play,' he explained later, 'and I was going to play that way. That's the only time that ever happened, someone telling me to play differently from the way I wanted to.'[27] For the rest of his life he harboured a grudge against 'that bitch, Henderson's wife'.

Most of Lester's time with Henderson was spent on the road, but he did get to experience something of life in New York City. During his first few days, when not rehearsing or undergoing re-education at the hands of Leora Henderson, he would wander abroad in search of a jam session. On one of these nights he encountered Billie Holiday, a nineteen-year-old singer virtually unknown outside Harlem. Thus began an extraordinary relationship which would last intermittently until the end of their lives, and which would cause their names to be forever linked. Everyone who knew them at the time, and has spoken about the matter subsequently, agrees on one thing: the relationship was entirely platonic. Billie went for dominant, masterful men, which Lester certainly wasn't. As we have seen, he was shy and unassertive, whereas she was street-wise, quick-tempered and open-hearted. By all accounts, she treated him rather like a younger brother, although he was six years her senior.

Billie Holiday's life had been a hard one from the beginning. The identity of her father has never been finally established, although she firmly believed him to be Clarence Holiday, guitarist with Fletcher Henderson between 1928 and 1933. As a child in Baltimore, she had been passed around among her mother's relatives, none of whom really wanted her, and was often cruelly neglected. Her mother, Sadie, combined domestic service with a little prostitution on the side, leaving the child alone for long periods. At the age of eleven she was sexually abused by a neighbour. The rapist was caught and sentenced and Billie was sent to a Roman Catholic children's home, the only stable home life she ever experienced. Her first job was as a domestic servant in a brothel, where she first heard the music of Louis Armstrong, Bessie Smith and other jazz pioneers on the Victrola. At fourteen, Billie moved with her mother to New York, where mother and daughter began working as five-dollar whores along Lenox Avenue. Billie was arrested, charged with vagrancy and served 100 days at a reformatory on Blackwell's Island.

Sadie got a job in the kitchen of a Harlem club patronised mainly by entertainers and musicians, where Billie joined her on her release, serving at the tables and occasionally singing. Fortunately, she was being heard by people who knew what they were listening to. Her name began to be passed around in Harlem musical circles and, at seventeen, she found herself a professional singer, albeit on the lowest rung of the ladder. Accounts of Billie at the time all say the same thing: she drank, smoked pot, laughed a lot, made lewd jokes and could sit listening to music with rapt attention for hours on end. Harlem knew about Billie Holiday long before the rest of the world. There was something special about her singing. It had the severe elegance of Louis Armstrong's trumpet, combined with an airy lightness, and it never sought to ingratiate itself through counterfeit gaiety or coquettish tricks.

On that first night, Billie sang and Lester played. 'From then on Lester knew how I used to love to have him come around and blow pretty solos behind me. So whenever he could, he'd come by the joints where I was singing, to hear me or to sit in.'[28] Together, they smoked prodigious quantities of cannabis and drank a fearsome concoction of their own devising, which they called 'top and bottom' – one half gin and one half port. He called her 'Lady Day' and she called him 'Prez'. 'The greatest man around then was Franklin D. Roosevelt and he was the President. So I started calling him "President". It got shortened to "Prez", but it still means what it was meant to mean.'[29]

This account has been challenged by Douglas Henry Daniels, who reports that several former members of the Blue Devils claimed to have been calling Lester 'Prez' before he even met Billie Holiday. This is possible, since Billie's ghost-written autobiography is not the most reliable of sources. However, her version long ago assumed the status of official legend, so perhaps the best course would be to follow John Ford's advice in *The Man Who Shot Liberty Valence*: 'When the legend becomes truth, print the legend'. Lester Young was known by a variety of names during his life. People used to call him 'Red' in the early Kansas City days, while to his family he was known as 'Bubba' or 'Uncle Bubba', and he would sometimes jocularly refer to himself as 'Doctor Willis Wiggins'.

Lester was finding it harder and harder to bear his pariah status in the Henderson band. He stuck it out for almost four months. Most of the time was spent on tour, although there was a week at the Apollo Theatre in Harlem at the beginning of June. Then, in July, the band found itself becalmed in New York when an expected residency fell through, and Lester decided he'd had enough. His way of resigning was absolutely typical. In order to dispel any notion that he had been sacked, he asked Henderson to write him a reference. 'I went to Fletcher and I said, "Will you give me a nice recommendation? I'll go back to Kansas City." And he says, "Oh, yeah!" right quick. "Thank you".'[30] If there was a note of uncon-cealed relief in Henderson's reply, it was because he had been working himself up to the unpleasant task of firing Lester in any case. At the same time, he was upset by the way Lester had been treated. He called the other three members of the reed section together and told them: 'It looks like I'm going to have to let this boy go, because he'll never have any peace around here with you. But I just want to tell you something before he goes – he can outplay you, and you, and you. And you're going to hear about him!'[31] The targets of this unprecedented outburst by the mild-mannered Fletcher Henderson were not just anonymous journeymen; they were Buster Bailey, Hilton Jefferson and Russell Procope, all musi-cians of considerable experience and reputation, whose *amour propre* would have taken a well-deserved knock.

Lester would probably never have to show his 'nice recommendation' to anyone, but that wasn't the point. On paper, at least, it proved he had not been fired. In fact, he became one half of an amicable exchange between Henderson and Andy Kirk. Lester left Henderson and joined Andy Kirk's Clouds of Joy, while Ben Webster left Kirk and joined Henderson. During his two months with Kirk, Lester reached his twenty-fifth birthday. So far, despite his experience and growing reputation, he had still not, apparently, seen the inside of a recording studio. There is a suggestion that he may have played alto on a record by Clarence Williams, made in June 1934, but it is impossible to prove because there is no saxophone solo. Once again, it is hugely frustrating, when everyone else's early years are represented by at least a few recorded snatches, that all we have of Lester Young in his youthful prime are the memories of dead people.

Leaving Kirk in September, perhaps because he didn't feel comfortable in Ben Webster's old place, he returned to Minneapolis, where he joined Rook Ganz's band, and later Boyd Atkins. It was steady work, but well beneath his level. It was probably frustration which drove him back to Kansas City after six months, with no job in prospect. Kansas City and its nightlife had become such a magnet for musicians and entertainers that it was overflowing with talent and he was obliged to take whatever casual engagements he could get. On the other hand, the standard was sky-high and jam sessions ubiquitous. Whatever happened, Lester knew he wouldn't starve. Two of the favourite jam-session spots, the Sunset and the Subway, were run by one Piney Brown, a friend to musicians and all-round good egg. As well as being *persona grata* with Pendergast's boys, and therefore able to do more or less as he liked, he was a dedicated music lover, and provided free food and drink for any musicians who cared to drop by and sit in with the band. Needless to say, his joints were always packed with musicians, particularly in the early part of the week, alternately playing and eating. Whenever old KC hands from those days got together, the name of Piney Brown would soon come up, always mentioned with affection. A regular job finally materialized at the Yellow Front Saloon. It lasted for a few months, after which Lester moved back to Minneapolis.

Installed once more in Rook Ganz's band, he must have been wondering whether he would ever get anywhere at all. He had not come within hailing distance of the Big Time, except for the stint with Henderson – and look how that had turned out. It was at this moment, when the outlook seemed particularly depressing, that he caught a late-night show on the radio. It came live from the Reno Club, Kansas City, and it featured Count Basie and his Barons of Rhythm. Everything about the band sounded wonderful to him – the loose, four-in-a-bar swing, the solos, the simple, jumping band riffs – everything except the tenor saxophonist, Slim Freeman. At least, that's how Lester later described it. It may well be that nobody with a job he coveted would have sounded much good to Lester Young. Whatever the case, he decided to do something uncharacteristically forceful. He fired off a cable to Basie, proposing himself for the job. And Basie accepted. 'So I joined Basie. It was very nice, just like I thought it would be.'[32]

3 'well, okay. so now we'll find out what happens'

In February 1936, when Lester Young joined him at the Reno Club, Bill Basie was thirty-one years old. Born in Red Bank, New Jersey, he had been a protégé of the great Fats Waller when they were both still teenagers. Indeed, he had literally sat at Waller's feet, observing those extremities as they worked the organ pedals in the pit of New York's Lincoln Theater. After a while, Fats entrusted him with the occasional interval spot on the organ and began passing on piano-playing jobs at Harlem rent parties. Before he was out of his teens, Basie was touring as a professional pianist with vaudeville shows. He would have been playing the 'stride' style, which had developed out of ragtime and was still quite formal and metronomic in its approach. The blues, of which he was to become such a consummate master, had not yet penetrated the black popular music of New York and the north-east. Nevertheless, to play stride even passably well required a more than adequate technique and, to the end of his life, Basie could produce occasional bursts of stride piano that would not have disgraced the mighty Fats himself.

Basie wound up in Kansas City when the Gonzelle White Show, with which he was touring, hit rock bottom and foundered there in 1927. This was where he made contact with the Blue Devils, whose blues-inflected music had such a dramatic effect on him. 'You just couldn't help wishing you were part of it', he recalled fondly in his autobiography. Within a year he actually *was* part of it, and part of Bennie Moten's orchestra when the Blue Devils were no more. He split from Moten for a while to form his own band, but returned later. Then, in April 1935, Moten suddenly died, the victim of a surgical mishap during a routine operation. Basie secured himself a job at the Reno Club and gradually gathered a little band of Blue Devils and Moten survivors around him. Throughout most of his long life, it was Basie's habit to act as the bewildered and innocent victim of fate, which had somehow landed him in the unlooked-for position of bandleader. He played the role to perfection, but the building of the Reno band was a skilful and determined piece of work. First, he persuaded the owner, Sol Steibold, to enlarge the band from six to nine pieces – three brass, three reeds, three rhythm ('three, three and three'). Then he located the scattered individuals he wanted, after which he was forced to sack the men whose places they were to take. Eventually, once Lester and drummer Jo Jones were aboard, seven of the nine were Blue Devils/Moten alumni.

> The Reno was not one of those big fancy places where you go in and go downstairs and all that. It was like a club off the street. But once you got inside, it was a cabaret, with a little bandstand and a little space for a floorshow, and with a bar up front, and there was also a little balcony in there. There were also girls available as dancing partners. It was a good place to work.[1]

The bandstand was so small that Basie's piano had to be placed on the floor, and a hole had to be cut in the ornamental shell above the stage in order to accommodate Walter Page's double bass. The hours were quite unbelievable by modern standards: 9pm to 5am, consisting of four floorshows of an hour's duration each, with dancing in between. For this they were paid $18 a week each (Basie got $21), plus tips. After work on Sundays, musicians would get together for what they called a 'Spook Breakfast' and, thus refreshed, would proceed to the delights of a jam session.

Lester had finally landed in the perfect environment. A nine-piece band in which everyone shares the same background and speaks the same musical language can do wonders, especially if it works the kind of hours that Basie's Barons of Rhythm were used to. Raised in territory bands, kept up to the mark by frequent jam sessions, they possessed a vast store of musical knowledge and customary practice. They could slip effortlessly into riff patterns, piling one on top of another, switch from unison to harmony and back again, drop back to let the rhythm section tick over for a chorus, pass solos around. Such written arrangements as they had were mainly created by Buster Smith, known as 'Prof', who led the saxophone section, but mostly the band played 'head arrangements', routines worked out collectively on the bandstand. Basie was delighted that his plan for the band had worked so well, especially the saxophone section of Prof, Lester and Jack Washington. 'I don't think we had over four or five sheets of music up there at that time. But we had our own thing, and we could always play some more blues and call it something, and we did our thing on the old standards and the current pops. We had a ball every night in there.'[2]

True to form, Basie always claimed that the extent of his ambition had been to 'get a group of guys together and work in a place like that and have some fun'. Everything that happened subsequently, he implied, was mere accident and good fortune. If so, it was a remarkable stroke of luck which caused the Reno Club to have been fitted up with a live radio link. Network radio, the first truly universal medium of entertainment, had developed with remarkable speed during the early 1930s, and one of its most popular features was the live relay of dance music from night-clubs, hotels and ballrooms. The nightly broadcast from the Reno went out over a local Kansas City station, W9XBY, which had an exceptionally powerful transmitter. Late at night, when most other local stations had closed down, leaving the airwaves clear, it could be picked up hundreds of miles away.

At this point the ubiquitous figure of John Hammond enters the picture once more. It is impossible to delve into the history of jazz and popular music without sooner or later encountering him, usually taking an active role in some important new development. Born in 1910, Hammond was a son of the American aristocracy. His paternal grand-father had been General Sherman's chief-of-staff during the Civil War, while his formidable mother was a descendant of Cornelius Vanderbilt, the steamship and railroad magnate. His twin passions were jazz and social reform, and when he came into his inheritance at the age of twenty-one he plunged ardently into both. With his money and social assurance he soon began to make his presence felt, writing articles in the press, seeking out new artists and sometimes even using his own money to pay for recording sessions. His tall, gangling figure, topped by his trademark crew cut, was likely to turn up anywhere that jazz was being performed. In 1936, he had already played a part in the burgeoning success of Benny Goodman and been instrumental in setting up Billie Holiday's first recording sessions. In the course of a long life he was to have a hand in advancing many other careers, including those of Basie, Charlie Christian, Aretha Franklin, Bob Dylan, George Benson and Bruce Springsteen.

On a cold January night in 1936, Hammond had been listening to Goodman's orchestra playing at the Congress Hotel in Chicago.

> I went out to my car, parked across the street from the Congress, not quite decided where to go next... I turned on the car radio... It was one o'clock in the morning. The local stations had all gone off the air and the only music I could find was at the top of the dial, 1550 kilocycles, where I picked up W9XBY... The nightly broadcast by the Count Basie band from the Reno Club was just beginning. I couldn't believe my ears... Basie had developed an extraordinary economy of style...using perfectly timed punctuations – a chord, even a single note – which could inspire a horn player to heights he had never reached before... Basie had discovered how effective simplicity can be.[3]

For Hammond, hearing something that excited him was enough to set him vigorously in motion. He was determined to do something about Basie. He began writing about the band in *Down Beat* and other journals, and advising everyone within earshot to tune in to the marvellous little band broadcasting from an obscure Kansas City nightspot. On a more practical level, he opened negotiations with Willard Alexander of the MCA agency, with a view to bringing Basie and the band to New York. He also secured an agreement in principle for a recording deal with the American Record Corporation. In 1936, the swing era was accelerating fast. The Depression was beginning to lift, more and more people were dancing and the demand for exciting new bands seemed insatiable. Inevitably, other music-business operators began to take an interest in Hammond's discovery. First off the mark was the notoriously pugnacious Joe Glaser, Louis Armstrong's manager and head of the United Booking Corporation, who turned up one night at the Reno. He was unimpressed by the band and Basie's quiet, undemonstrative style, but took a fancy to Hot Lips Page, the ebullient trumpet soloist. He made Page an offer he couldn't refuse and Page gave in his notice. By now, Basie had learned of Hammond's efforts on his behalf, and realized that big things might be brewing. He was not surprised, therefore, when Dave Kapp, of Decca Records, appeared in Kansas City, claiming to be an emissary from John Hammond and waving a recording contract. It seemed like the break of a lifetime. Basie signed, and that night he told Lester Young the news.

> I called him over, got us a couple of nips and went and stood outside the doorway to the back alley, where we usually went when we wanted to have a little private sip and a little personal chat.
>
> 'Well,' I said. 'I got some great news. I think we'll take a Pullman into Chicago and do some recording for Decca.'
>
> And all he did was just sort of stand there looking into space like he hadn't heard what I'd said... Then he looked at me again.
>
> 'What did I hear you say? Did I hear you?'
>
> 'Yes,' I said. 'We're going to Chicago to make some records for Decca.'... And he just stood there, nodding his head, thinking about it, and then the next thing he said was like he was talking to himself.
>
> 'Well, okay. So now we'll find out what happens.'[4]

A few days later, John Hammond finally made the journey to Kansas City and presented himself at the Reno. Basie greeted him warmly.

'A friend of yours was here to see me, John.'

'Who?' I asked. 'I didn't send anyone.'

'Dave Kapp.'

'Let me see what you signed,' I said, fearing the worst.[5]

His fears were justified. The contract called for twenty-four 78 rpm sides a year, for three years, at a total fee of $750 each year. It contained no provision for payment of royalties on sales and was totally binding on Basie's part. To Basie, with his $21 dollars a week, plus tips, it seemed like a lot of money, but $750 wouldn't even cover the session fees for the musicians, at the minimum rate stipulated by the American Federation of Musicians (AFM). Hammond later went to the AFM and succeeded in getting the fee raised to the session minimum, but he could do nothing at all about the lack of royalties.

In all other respects, however, his visit to Kansas City was full of glorious revelations. In the first place, he couldn't believe that a ten-piece band (Basie had managed to add another trumpet) could create such a full and varied sound. Neither could he believe the hours they worked and the enthusiasm they succeeded in maintaining. But most of all he couldn't believe Lester Young. He already knew, from the Henderson episode, what an exceptional musician Lester was, but he only fully appreciated the extent of his talent when he joined Lester on his early-morning prowl in search of a jam session, which they found at 'a joint on 18th Street'.

> He would launch himself headlong into improvisations which, with each new chorus, renewed themselves as if by magic; it was as though his energy and originality knew no bounds. Lester could improvise on the same theme for an hour at a stretch, without once giving the impression that he might be running out of ideas... His features evinced not the slightest emotion and his whole being was concentrated in the music.[6]

The agency agreement with Willard Alexander and MCA went through without a hitch. Basie's band was to be enlarged to fourteen players, to put it on a par with other leading bands, and the 'Barons of Rhythm' tag was dropped in favour of a simple 'Count Basie and his Orchestra'. There was a panic when Buster Smith, 'Prof', announced that he would not be coming along. The whole enterprise seemed far too risky to him and, anyway, life was fine in KC and the south-west and he saw no reason to uproot himself. They all tried to persuade him but he would not budge, and a replacement lead alto was eventually found in the form of Caughey Roberts. The enlargement process brought in a number of musicians destined to play an important part in Basie's future success, in particular trumpeter Buck Clayton, and Herschel Evans returned to the fold, his gloriously fat, oily tenor saxophone tone striking a perfect contrast with Lester's.

The new band was booked to open at the Grand Terrace, Chicago, on 6 November 1936. They played a Halloween Night ball at the Paseo Hall in Kansas City on 31 October, and were all set to go, when Walter Page announced that his wife was unhappy about the whole thing and he might have to cry off. Since its rhythm section was probably the band's strongest suit, and Walter Page (known as 'Big 'Un') was its mainstay, this was potentially disastrous news. Everyone pleaded with Mrs Page, even promising to send Big 'Un back once they had got established, and she finally relented. Thirteen of them set off for Chicago: trumpeters Buck Clayton, Joe Keyes and Carl 'Tatti' Smith; trombonists Dan Minor and George Hunt; saxophonists Caughey Roberts, Lester Young, Herschel Evans and Jack Washington; Basie on piano, Walter Page on bass, Jo Jones on drums and vocalist Jimmy Rushing. The final member, guitarist and violinist Claude 'Fiddler' Williams, would join them at their destination.

It was not the most triumphant of debuts. In fact, it was distinctly underwhelming. The Grand Terrace was nothing like the Reno Club. It had a large stage, a proper dance floor, a fully produced stage show, subdued lighting, mirrored walls, hat-check girls, girls selling cigarettes and flowers – in short, all the trappings of sophistication as portrayed in Hollywood films of the period and reproduced for the delectation of patrons at 3955 South Parkway, Chicago, Ill. The main problem was the show, for which they were handed a pile of music and expected to play it, which most of them couldn't do. Left to themselves, they could have played all night, non-stop, but faced with tangos, waltzes, unfamiliar ballad selections and excerpts from the *Poet And Peasant* overture, they were at something of a disadvantage. According to Basie, the customers, once they had got used to the band's style, were happy enough, but there was no denying that the floorshow was a shambles. The vocalists and 'speciality' acts (jugglers, acrobats, etc.) complained so bitterly that the boss, Ed Fox, was ready to fire the band, but the showgirls and chorus dancers loved the rhythm Basie's men were laying down, and stuck up for them. Basie overheard one dancer, Alma Smith, berating Fox: 'Why don't you just lay off... Take it easy. These are just a nice group of country boys. They just come to town. This is all new to them... One of these days you might be trying like hell to get them back in here, just wait and see. And I hope to God I'm still living to see them turn you down!' Then she took Basie aside and told him, 'Don't you worry. Just play something behind me'.[7] Fortunately, because of his apprenticeship in travelling outfits like the Gonzelle White Show, 'playing something' on piano for show-dancers came as second nature to Bill Basie.

And so they managed to struggle through, but it was a gruesome few weeks. Given all the advance publicity, it was inevitable that the press would take an interest in the band's Chicago debut, and most of the critics seem to have taken the same view as the Grand Terrace management. 'By the time you read this', one wrote, 'they will be on their way back to Kansas City.' George T. Simon, reviewing a live broadcast from the Grand Terrace for *Metronome* magazine, was particularly trenchant: 'If you think the sax section sounds out of tune, catch the brass! And if you think the brass by itself is out of tune, catch the intonation of the band as a whole!! Swing is swing, but music is music, too.'[8] By dint of much rehearsal, and with the help of a pile of arrangements generously lent by Horace Henderson, Fletcher's brother, matters gradually improved, but some problems were endemic. Musicians who had scarcely been earning a living wage could not afford new instruments, nor could they pay for the professional maintenance of those they had. All brass and reed players acquire the skills of basic instrumental make-do-and-mend, involving rubber bands, string, bits of cork etc., but these are only stop-gap measures. Basie's men were mostly playing instruments that no further patching could improve, with the inevitable result, cruelly highlighted by George T. Simon, that they played out of tune. Again, one of the glories of this early Basie band was its ability, perfected at the Reno Club, to create coherent music by ear, employing instinct and a shared vocabulary. Some, like Lester and Buck Clayton, could read well, but most couldn't. Now that there were fourteen of them, and they were having to keep up with the latest dance tunes and popular songs, the good old method was no longer sufficient. To use a modern cliché, Count Basie and his Orchestra were on a steep learning curve, and there were bound to be casualties eventually.

The first recording sessions under the Decca contract did not, after all, take place in Chicago. No doubt it was felt that a longer playing-in period was called for. This gave John Hammond the opportunity he had been waiting for, the chance to have some small revenge on Decca for stealing the Basie band from under his nose. He was determined to get in first and record, if not the full band, then some of its leading members, especially Lester Young. On 9 November 1936, a couple of days after the Grand Terrace opening, a small band gathered at the Chicago studios of the American Record Corporation. It consisted of Basie, Walter Page, Jo Jones, Lester Young and trumpeter Carl 'Tatti' Smith. Hammond had wanted Buck Clayton, but he had fallen victim to the trumpet player's occupational hazard, a split lip. Jimmy Rushing was also there, to provide the vocals. The time was 10am, not so much an early morning as a late night, since none of them had yet been to bed.

This was the moment when Lester Young finally sidled out of the shadows, the moment when he ceased to be just a name, a rumour from the territory, a set of tall tales concerning jam sessions in bars and hotel lobbies and shoeshine parlours, and became a sound. For the first time, his music was caught, frozen onto shellac grooves and sent out into the world. Forty-five years later, after a lifetime in the record business, Hammond could still categorically say of those three hours, 'It's the only perfect, completely perfect recording session I've ever had anything to do with.'[9]

They recorded four pieces that morning, the first being 'Shoe Shine Boy', a cheerful little tune from the 1930 musical show *Hot Chocolates*. Basie and the rhythm section play an introduction, setting tempo and mood, and then, after forty-five seconds, Lester Young bursts forth. The first impression is of blazing energy and complete self-assurance. He plays with all the confidence and poise of a young man fully aware of his powers and in complete control of them. The only possible comparison is with the young Louis Armstrong of ten years earlier. Faced with such unhesitating fluency, it is easy to understand why other musicians at jam sessions would simply lay down their instruments and sit goggle-eyed. 'Look, I didn't come here to give a concert', he had complained, but who could possibly hope to follow this? It is easy to believe, too, that he could keep it up for hours on end. Here, constrained by the three-minute limit of the ten-inch, 78 rpm record, he confines himself to two choruses, sixty-four bars, lasting exactly one minute, but it is obvious that he has barely got into his stride. The take was a perfect one, but, perhaps unable to believe what they had just heard, Hammond and the engineer called for a second. Lester plays another two choruses, completely different but equally inventive and energetic. And this is a man who has already been playing all night and would otherwise be on his way to bed.

Nothing becomes Lester Young so well as his first utterance on record, a phrase eight bars long, starting and finishing with exactly the same interval, C to F in quavers (eighth-notes). The notes themselves are all perfectly straightforward. All but three of them are contained in the scale of F major, and if you write them down you end up with eight bars of harmless-looking crotchets (quarter-notes) and quavers, with not even a triplet to ruffle the surface. So why, when you try to hum or whistle those eight bars, does it take half-a-dozen attempts to get them right? Simple and tricky at the same time. Devious candour, one of the unique qualities of Lester Young's imagination, stands revealed in these first few seconds of his recorded work.

After the two takes of 'Shoe Shine Boy', they tackled 'Evenin'', a minor-key song of no great distinction by Harry White and Mitchell Parish, to feature Jimmy Rushing. Lester plays no solo here, apart from eight bars in the opening instrumental chorus. The main focus is on Rushing, whose high, plaintive but at the same time lusty voice was to be a vital component of Basie's music for many years to come. He had been a member of both the Blue Devils and Moten's orchestra, and no one embodies more clearly the proclivity of south-western musicians to turn any tune into a species of blues. Every phrase is flooded with blues inflexions and he imbues 'Evenin'' with a rising passion that its authors can never have envisaged. Rushing follows this with a real blues, the kind of thing that might have been heard issuing nightly from any of the joints around 12th and Vine Streets in Kansas City. Here called 'Boogie-Woogie', it is simply a comfortable assemblage of traditional blues elements – the rolling boogie piano of the title, four venerable verses from Rushing ('Baby, what's on your worried mind?' etc.), simple riffs from Lester and Tatti Smith, and a two-chorus solo by Lester, so plain and lucid as to defy comment or analysis.

The final number of the session is 'Lady Be Good' (or 'Oh! Lady Be Good', to be strictly correct), from the 1924 musical comedy of the same name by George and Ira Gershwin, although the original melody doesn't get much of a look-in. The pattern is very similar to that of 'Shoe Shine Boy', with Lester taking the first main solo. Once again, the actual notes are simple, but they are deployed with such rhythmic cunning that every phrase contains a surprise.[10]

Having now heard him at some length, we can begin to understand what it was about Lester Young that had caused such consternation in the Henderson ranks. Anything less like Coleman Hawkins it would be difficult to imagine. When the discs from the session were released a few months later, under the band name 'Jones-Smith Incorporated', they were greeted at first with baffled silence, because this was simply not the way the tenor saxophone was supposed to sound. The most obvious difference lay in the tone, but tone is just one element of style, inseparable from others, such as articulation, phrasing, and ultimately personality itself. Hawkins played the way he did because that's the way he was. Most other tenor saxophone players, even if they shared no personality traits at all with him, strove to play as though they did. It never occurred to Lester to follow such a course. From remarks he made at various times in his life, it is clear that he couldn't understand why anyone should want to.

Lester's tone is not thin or weak. It is certainly not, as some claimed at the time, the result of failing to breathe from the diaphragm. Anyone who has ever tried filling five feet of tenor saxophone with air will know that it simply cannot be done without steady pressure from that organ. Lester's tone is supported by just as much air as Hawkins's. Indeed, listening to 'Lady Be Good' and 'Shoe Shine Boy', one has the impression that the process starts somewhere in the region of his boots. Hawkins's forceful manner and ornate conception led him to develop a sound that was not only broad but biting. It had what saxophonists call 'edge'. By contrast, Lester's sound at this period was round and contained, with virtually no edge at all. It didn't cut, it floated. It was this quality in Trumbauer which had first attracted him, and he had been working on it ever since.

As he tottered off to get some sleep, at around the time when solid citizens were sitting down to their lunch, he must have been wondering about the future. He was twenty-seven years old and a corner had at last been turned. 'Well okay. So now we'll find out what happens.'

4 'the hippest thing I ever heard'

Basie's Grand Terrace engagement ended on 3rd December and the band travelled to Buffalo, NY, on the first leg of a tour through the New England winter that was to occupy most of that month. On the night they played New London, Connecticut, a blizzard was raging and the ballroom was only a quarter-full. Eventually, they reached New York in time for their Christmas Eve debut at Roseland, Manhattan's most popular ballroom. Although Roseland had a policy of booking both black and white bands, its clientele was exclusively white and totally unfamiliar with the kind of music Basie represented. The band had been given a big publicity build-up, which Basie admitted made him nervous. In his autobiography, he recounts a meeting with Roseland's amiable manager, Joe Belford. 'He poured us a little nip, and we had a couple. He said not to worry about anything. Just take it easy. Just go ahead. And then, when was I walking out the door, he called after me, "*And don't forget the tangos!* "....It was not as bad as the Grand Terrace, which was the worst, but we were definitely not a hit in the Roseland either.'[1]

It was not unusual at the time for bands to find themselves booked into thoroughly unsuitable venues, playing to people who turned out to be, at best, indifferent and, at worst, positively hostile. This was particularly the case with new bands, black or white, before they had become known for their own style of music. Benny Goodman had been floundering around obscure hotel ballrooms, close to bankruptcy, before his sudden success with a young west-coast audience in 1935. Woody Herman, on stage at a ballroom in Texas, was handed a furious note from the manager, demanding that he 'stop playing those nigger blues'. For Basie, the smart Chatterbox Room at Pittsburgh's William Penn Hotel proved similarly sticky:

> The people were sitting in there eating dinner. Clink...clink...clink...and we hit and WHAM! And everything froze right in place just like in the movies. The waiters came to a cold stop right wherever they were... I could see the expression on their faces... What the hell did we know

about playing for dinner? We'd never even been in a room like that, let alone knowing how to play in there.[2]

Basie finished at Roseland on 20 January 1937 and the following day saw the band's first recording session under the Decca contract. The very first piece recorded under the name 'Count Basie and his Orchestra' was Fats Waller's 'Honeysuckle Rose', and it's as good an example as any of the original Basie method. It opens with two choruses from Basie himself, the first sticking close to the melody, in simple but fully voiced stride style, the second quoting briefly from another Waller tune, 'A Handful Of Keys'. At the end of the second chorus Lester enters with a two-bar break, neatly effecting a key-change from F to D-flat, and takes a high-spirited chorus, not quite in the 'Shoe Shine Boy' class, but elegant nonetheless. We are now more than half-way through the number and the full band has not played a note yet. The brass and saxophone sections come in for just two choruses, mainly superimposed riffs, with an eight-bar passage for the rhythm section and another for Buck Clayton, and the piece ends. Constrained within the three-minute confines of a ten-inch disc, 'Honeysuckle Rose' may come across as somewhat desultory, but a structure as open-ended as this would have been perfect for a place like the Reno Club. One can imagine it going on indefinitely, with solos passed around the band and riffs being cooked up ad infinitum.

These very early Basie records are fascinating, in that they feature two distinct types of arrangement, the loose, KC riff kind, described above, and the full orchestrations that were being added as quickly as possible. As we shall see, it took some time to resolve this awkward duality. In retrospect, numbers in the former style still sound fresh and exciting, while many of the latter have grown a little quaint with the passing years. The next piece to be recorded is one of the second type, a version of 'Pennies From Heaven' as a vocal feature for Jimmy Rushing, from the pen of veteran arranger Don Redman. Apart from Basie's piano, the band sounds pretty anonymous. It also sounds far more technically efficient than earlier reports had suggested. Clearly, a lot of rehearsal had been taking place – necessary but tedious, especially to an efficient sight-reader like Lester Young. The only complaint he ever voiced about a band in which he was otherwise deeply happy concerned rehearsals.

> In Basie's band there always would be someone who didn't know his part. Seems to me that if a musician can't read, he should say so, and then you can help him. Or you give him his part before. But Basie wouldn't. I used to talk to him about it, but he had no eyes for it. You had to sit there and play it over and over and over again. Just sit in that chair.[3]

Basie was so attached to the old Kansas City methods that he stuck to them even when he had replaced the weak links. The trombonist Dickie Wells, describing his audition for the band in 1938, provides a fascinating insider's account:

> 'Come on,' said Basie, 'take your axe out and sit down and blow with the cats. See if you like it.'
>
> 'Where's my music?' I asked.
>
> 'Sit in and see what happens,' he said...
>
> Basie would start out and vamp a little, set a tempo and call out, 'That's it!' He'd set a rhythm for the saxes first and Earl Warren would pick that up and lead the saxes. Then he'd set one for the bones [trombones] and we'd pick that up. Now it's our rhythm against theirs. The third rhythm would be for the trumpets and they'd start fanning their Derbies...
>
> The solos would fall between the ensembles, but that's how the piece would begin, and that's how Basie put his tunes together. He had a big band, but he handled it as though it were six pieces.
>
> 'Am I hired?' I asked him.
>
> 'I didn't fire you, did I?' was his answer.[4]

And that's how the remaining two numbers at the session of 20 January, 'Swinging At The Daisy Chain' and 'Roseland Shuffle', both credited as Basie compositions, first saw the light of day. The latter is a kind of duet feature for Basie and Lester, in which two-thirds of the playing time consists of the pair of them playfully exchanging four-bar phrases.

Three weeks at Roseland were followed by a week at the Paramount Theater, so members of Basie's band had an uninterrupted month in which to get established in New York. Lester immediately resumed his practice of touring the late-night spots in search of jam sessions, and soon ran into Billie Holiday again. From that moment, Prez and Lady Day became a kind of after-hours double act. Wherever she was singing, he was likely to turn up sooner or later and join her on stage. He had taken a room at the Hotel Theresa in Harlem but, after discovering a rat in his shirt drawer, left and moved in for a while with Billie and her mother, Sadie, whom he christened 'Duchess'. Sadie was normally hostile to any man that Billie brought home, indeed to men in general, but seems to have taken to Lester. Like others who knew them well, she understood that there was no sexual dimension to his friendship with her daughter. It may have been at around this time that a faint but persistent rumour began to circulate, hinting that Lester was homosexual. He was quiet and mild-mannered, he walked with a stealthy, tiptoe gait, his voice as a young man was soft, light in texture and fairly high-pitched, and he was the only man regularly seen around with Billie who wasn't forever putting his hands on her. When the rumour finally came to his notice, his only comment was, 'I never even auditioned!' Quite soon, indeed, he formed a relationship with a white woman, a nurse named Mary Dale, and they eventually set up home together.

Billie's career, like Lester's, had suffered a few false starts. In 1933, she had recorded a couple of numbers with a small band under Benny Goodman's leadership, and in the following year appeared in *Symphony in Black*, a short film featuring Duke Ellington's orchestra. Neither of these had made much impression, but over the past year and a half she had begun to enjoy a modest success. Perhaps inevitably, John Hammond was behind it. He had discovered her in 1933, singing in a Harlem speakeasy, and had done his best to promote her career ever since. An opportunity presented itself with the advent of the jukebox in 1934. Within a year there was scarcely a bar, drugstore or hotel lobby in the USA without one of these machines, and Hammond realized that there was very little material on them to appeal to African-American tastes. He succeeded in persuading Harry Grey, head of Brunswick Records, that here was an untapped market. He proposed recording popular songs of the day in jam-session style, featuring a vocalist and six or seven instrumentalists. With no need for elaborate arrangements the production costs would be low, as little as $250–300 a session. 'It astonishes me', he recalled forty years later, 'how casually we were able to assemble such all-star groups... Compared to the kind of money that's around today, they all came for scale'.[5] 'Scale', the basic union rate, was $20.

In a back-handed kind of way, this was the perfect recipe for making jazz records, and a flourishing sub-industry soon established itself. It worked well because, for the past ten years or so, jazz and popular song had been speaking the same language, ever since Louis Armstrong had instituted a grammar and syntax for jazz improvisation – a fluid line, derived from a recognizable melody and its underlying harmonic sequence, deployed over a regular beat. Form presented no problem. The American popular song chorus was almost invariably thirty-two bars long and cast in one of two shapes, either four eight-bar segments, with the third segment, usually called the 'bridge' or 'middle eight', providing contrast (A/A/B/A), or two sixteen-bar segments, in which the second segment is a variation of the first (Ai/Aii). It is unlikely that anyone involved considered the matter in these theoretical terms, any more than they gave a thought to the grammatical basis of their everyday speech, but it added up to a wonderfully simple and malleable idiom.

The key figure in Hammond's plan was the pianist Teddy Wilson. Assured, urbane, tasteful, a great fashioner of adroit introductions and apt comments on the side, Wilson was the perfect accompanist and a superb leader of small bands. He had a particular skill in shaping a performance to fit neatly into the three minutes of a ten-inch record side, while retaining a feeling of relaxed informality. The format proved highly successful, eventually earning its own little brand-name, 'swing-sing'. Apart from Billie Holiday, the featured vocalists included Mildred Bailey, Helen Ward, Midge Williams, Nan Wynn and the young Ella Fitzgerald. There was no shortage of musicians for Wilson to choose from, either. Every top band spent time in New York City and sooner or later leading soloists with Fletcher Henderson, Duke Ellington, Jimmie Lunceford, Benny Goodman and others would check in to earn $20 for three hours' pleasant employment. Now that Basie's band was on the scene, Hammond lost no time in bringing Lester Young, Buck Clayton *et al* into this charmed circle. The date was 25 January 1937 and the band, billed on the record label as 'Teddy Wilson & his Orchestra', consisted of Wilson himself, Lester, Buck, Benny Goodman (appearing, for contractual reasons, under the pseudonym 'Shoeless John Jackson'), Walter Page, Jo Jones, guitarist Freddie Green – and Billie Holiday.

By all accounts, the atmosphere in the studio was exceptionally warm and friendly, despite the fact that the four Basie players had never met the other three before. There is certainly no sense of strain in the music, even though the first two pieces may have presented something of a challenge. They are both songs by Irving Berlin, and neither conforms strictly to the pattern outlined above. The first, 'He Ain't Got Rhythm', takes the form Ai/B/Aii, the segment lengths, in bars, being 18/8/14. It is also a rather wordy song, and wordy songs were never Billie's forte, but the result is remarkably easy-sounding, especially Lester's eighteen-bar solo, following Billie's chorus. Small ensembles like this constitute the chamber music of the swing era, and in such surroundings his smooth tone and precise articulation create an impression of intimacy and directness that matches the occasion perfectly. The second piece, 'This Year's Kisses' (6/6/8/8), introduces us to one of his particular strengths, the ability to play a melody virtually straight yet make it sound utterly personal and confidential. It was a gift which never deserted him, and accounts for some of his most sublime moments. In this case, his theme statement is immediately followed by Billie, who further intensifies the mood. Her falling inflexions on the ends of the lines, 'This year's new romance / Doesn't seem to have a chance' render a very unremarkable couplet almost absurdly touching. Lester takes very little part in the next song to be recorded, 'Why Was I Born?', by Jerome Kern and Oscar Hammerstein II, but it is worth noting for Buck Clayton's elegant theme statement, the sense of spacious ease imparted by Billie's phrasing, and how much the notoriously jazz-hating Jerome Kern would have detested the whole thing. Finally, there is the near-masterpiece of this first Lester–Billie session, a version of 'I Must Have That Man', a song by Jimmy McHugh and Dorothy Fields. If we knew nothing of Lester Young's personality we should be able to deduce it from the expressive tenderness of his sixteen-bar solo here, following Billie's vocal chorus. In his work with Basie's band, Lester Young never had the opportunity to play like this, because romantic ballads were the preserve of Herschel Evans, so without this and other small-band sessions that whole aspect of his talent at this period would have been lost to us.

After its week at the Paramount, Basie's band moved on to the William Penn Hotel, Pittsburgh. Its Chatterbox Room, where, as we have learned, Basie's opening set apparently left both diners and waiters in a state of shock, was provided with a radio link and, as luck would have it, some of the broadcasts were recorded. Thus, from February 1937, we have the first live recordings of the band actually at work. It is noticeable how much more broadly Lester plays here than in the studio. In those days it was not customary for soloists to step out in front of the band and play into a microphone. They merely stood up behind their music stands and delivered. The art of projecting a sound on a wind instrument is akin to the actor's art of projecting the voice, and it is now far less widely practised than it was. Modern public address systems and multiple microphones have brought huge and largely unrecognized changes in performance practice, changes which extend even to the instruments themselves. Saxophones manufactured in the 1930s, for instance, are appreciably heavier and more robust than their modern equivalents. In any case, the sheer lung-power exerted by Lester in his solos finally puts paid to any suggestion that he was a weak, wispy player.

The Chatterbox recordings also contain the only known example of Claude 'Fiddler' Williams actually playing the fiddle with Basie. Most of the time he played virtually inaudible guitar in the rhythm section, but he steps out here to deliver a lively fiddle solo on 'Lady Be Good'. His tenure, however, was nearly at an end. Hammond detested the use of the violin in jazz, and kept up a barrage of complaint about Fiddler's solo spots. Furthermore, Jo Jones and Big 'Un had been hugely impressed by Freddie Green's rhythm guitar playing when they'd encountered him for the first time on Billie's session, and were lobbying strongly for a change of guitarist. So Fiddler left after the Pittsburgh engagement. By a strange irony, he succeeded in outliving them all. He died in April 2004, aged ninety-six, the last surviving member of the original Count Basie orchestra. Fiddler's was not the only departure. There was a purge in the trumpet section, too. Tatti Smith and Joe Keyes both left in the same month, to be replaced by Ed Lewis and Bobby Moore. But the most spectacular new arrival was Billie Holiday.

Basie had never really considered hiring a female singer. He knew all about Billie from Lester, Buck and the others, but he had not heard her in person until Hammond took him to hear her at Monroe's Uptown House in Harlem. 'And she was something', Basie recalled in his auto-biography. 'A very, very attractive lady. And when she sang, it was an altogether different style. I hadn't heard anything like it and I was all for it.'[6] And so, with very little persuasion on either side, Billie came aboard what everybody concerned remembered as a happy ship. Not only were Billie and Lester close friends, she and Freddie Green were lovers. Many who knew them well asserted that the quiet, level-headed Green was the best man she ever attached herself to. The general opinion was that if she had stuck with him her life would have turned out very differently.

Billie joined the band at the quaintly named Enna Jettick Park, in Binghampton, NY, on 14 March 1937. Apart from occasional week-long engagements at theatres and ballrooms, much of life was lived on the road, travelling in a bus with a crooked chassis which, according to Jo Jones, 'used to go down the highway sideways'. Despite its growing repu-tation, Basie's band earned remarkably little money. In some ways, they were not much better off than the old Blue Devils had been. There was certainly not enough cash to pay retainers, which meant that musicians were paid by the job, had to find their own accommodation and pay their own living expenses. At $24 a gig, it was a hand-to-mouth existence. To live such a life you had to be young and you had to get on well together, which, on the whole, they did. One exception was Billie's instant and abiding dislike of Jimmy Rushing. This was not professional jealousy; it was simply that Rushing was exceedingly careful with his money, not to say miserly, whereas Billie was impulsively open handed. It was while travelling in the crabwise bus that she first shot dice. Lester asked her to roll the dice for him, to bring him luck. She did so and, despite not knowing the rules of the game, had an extraordinary run of winning shots and cleaned the other players out. Lester, on the other hand, never seemed to have any luck at all, despite being a keen dice-player. He was also a member of the band's baseball team, which played against other bands, including those of Harry James and Benny Goodman. Lester was the pitcher, which must have been a sight to see.

Unfortunately, Billie could not record with Basie, because they were under contract to separate companies. There are, however, three numbers on surviving off-air recordings, two from Harlem's Savoy Ballroom, broadcast live on 30 June 1937, and one from the Meadowbrook Lounge, Cedar Grove, NJ, dated 3 November 1937. The Savoy, 'The Home of Happy Feet', was an enormous place. The building itself occupied an entire city block on Lexington Avenue, between 140th and 141st Streets, and inside there was a vast dance floor with two full-sized bandstands on which bands would alternate. To sing a romantic love song in such circumstances could not have been easy, but Billie performs 'They Can't Take That Away From Me' with all the rhythmic subtlety she brought to her small-band recordings. Nevertheless, it is the throwaway dance number, 'Swing, Brother, Swing' in which she really excels. It lasts less than two minutes, but in that short space she manages not only to deliver a magisterial lesson in how to make a tune swing, but the sheer joy in her voice as she sings, 'And there ain't nobody gonna hold me down!' amounts almost to a definition of the swing era itself, which was then approaching its zenith.

The high-water mark of swing is often quoted as 16 January 1938, the night when Benny Goodman's band played at Carnegie Hall, the first non-classical concert to be held within those hallowed walls. A mock jam session was included as part of the show, with guest artists from the bands of Count Basie and Duke Ellington. The Basie contingent consisted of Lester, Buck, Basie, Freddie Green and Walter Page. Jazz concerts, as opposed to band-shows, were a rarity in those days, and a row of musicians stepping forward, one at a time, to play a string of solos on 'Honeysuckle Rose' was perhaps not the best way of introducing a slightly cautious audience to the idea of unstructured and unadorned jazz. The performance lasted just short of a quarter of an hour, which must have seemed interminable to people used to getting their swing in three-minute bursts. A recording of the concert, released many years later, reveals that Lester took the first solo, a bubbling two choruses that drew a hearty round of applause. Later that same night, the full Basie band appeared at the Savoy, in what the New York *Amsterdam News* reported as 'a wide-open battle of swing' with the incumbent Chick Webb orchestra. It says something for the devotion of Harlemites to their favourite bands, and to swing music in general, that the dance floor became too crowded for dancing and there were traffic jams on Lexington Avenue and surrounding streets. Although Webb, with his vocalist Ella Fitzgerald, was declared the winner by popular acclaim, the result was far closer than aficionados had predicted. Billie left the band a few weeks later, following a series of altercations with Willard Alexander – mainly, it seems, because he tried to give her advice on her repertoire and deportment. Not surprisingly, she told him what he could do with it.

Jazz music is unique in one important respect, namely that it was the first performed music to be widely recorded, and therefore not only preserved in time but heard beyond the culture which created it. Because of recording, the whole world can today listen to Lester Young playing with the Count Basie orchestra in 1938. This means that jazz recordings became definitive 'texts', and nowadays assume a position of prime importance to both performers and listeners. But this was not necessarily the case back in 1938. For Basie and other bandleaders, the instant medium of radio was far more important. Regular live radio exposure made a band's reputation and established what would now be called its 'fan base', and it was worth going to extreme lengths to acquire it. That is why Willard Alexander booked the band into the Famous Door, a small club on 52nd Street with a radio connection to the CBS network, in the summer of 1938. From all other points of view, it was a totally unsuitable venue. The bandstand was too small to take a fourteen-piece band and the audience capacity was sixty at most. Add to this the fact that New York City in summer can be unbearably hot and humid and you have a recipe for disaster. But so determined was Alexander to get Basie's band onto the airwaves that he paid for alterations to be made, and even for air conditioning to be installed. The impact of such a band in such a confined space must have been overwhelming. Certainly, the off-air recordings which survive are breathtaking in their intensity and heart-lifting in their *joie de vivre*. Furthermore, three broadcasts a week on a major network finally raised Basie unquestionably to the position of a 'name' bandleader, recognized across the United States.

The band even appeared in a movie, *Policy Man*, which was advertised with the tag-line 'Music! Action! Mystery! Thrills!' The film was almost certainly a low-budget second feature and all prints of it have long-since vanished, but from surviving documents it seems that members of the band, including Lester Young, Herschel Evans and Buck Clayton, were included in the cast credits.[7] A fleeting glimpse of the band, with Lester soloing, appears in a movie newsreel item about a swing event at Randall's Island, NY, dating from either July or September 1938. This clip has been incorporated in several television documentaries on jazz history.

All bandleaders were under constant siege by music publishers and song pluggers, trying to persuade or bribe them into recording their wares. A glance at his discography shows that Basie must have been unusually good at keeping these characters at bay, since the bulk of the list consists of good, Basie-style material, with remarkably few duds. But every man has his price, and Basie's was a pair of tickets to Yankee Stadium on 22 June 1938, when Joe Louis was to have his revenge on the German heavyweight, Max Schmeling. Basie got his tickets, Schmeling was duly put in his place, joy was unconfined among black Americans, and musical posterity was saddled with the most atrocious record of Basie's career, a piece entitled 'Mama Don't Want No Peas 'n' Rice 'n' Coconut Oil'. Even the versatile Jimmy Rushing could do nothing with it.

At the same time, although he was entirely unaware of it, Lester Young was gathering an army of admirers, both black and white, and mostly in their teens, who would form his own dedicated fan base in the years to come. Some of them would grow to become musicians in their turn. The late saxophonist Al Cohn remembered first hearing him as a 'jazz-minded' thirteen-year-old.

> When I heard him I thought it was the hippest thing I ever heard. The first thing that struck me was the sound. It was different from anybody else's sound — anybody else's approach to the tenor. Most of the tenor players played in the Coleman Hawkins style. This was a big, fat sound — large, dark sound. And Prez was so light. To me it was so effortless, and his harmonic approach was different, and his rhythmic approach, too — different from the way the other fellows were playing.[8]

And, along with the regular broadcasts, there were records for Lester's new followers to seek out, as Al Cohn fondly recalled: 'Then I began rummaging through the nine-cent bargain counters in those stores that sold used 78s... Well, when I heard 'Jumpin' At The Woodside' and 'Dark Rapture', I switched [from clarinet] overnight. Prez was the reason I became a saxophone player.'[9] On the other side of the country, in Los Angeles, Cohn's near-contemporary, Dexter Gordon, felt exactly the same: 'Hawk was a master of the horn, a musician who did everything possible with it, the right way. But when Prez appeared we all started listening to him alone. Prez had an entirely new sound, one that we seemed to have been waiting for.'[10]

Figure 4. 1939. Probably taken at a jam session (because he is not wearing a band uniform), this classic shot of Lester, aged thirty, shows not only the extraordinary angle at which he held the instrument, but his curious, lop-sided embouchure, possibly the result of uneven and sensitive teeth. (Frank Driggs collection)

Without doubt, this was the happiest time of Lester Young's life. He was installed, among friends, in a band which made the most of his talents – a band, moreover, that was playing better and better and growing steadily in public esteem. He had also acquired a reputation as a 'character', on account of his little eccentricities. Principal among these was his inventive and highly personal use of language. He is credited, for instance, with the first use of the word 'bread', to mean money, and probably also of 'cool' as a term of approval. To 'feel a draft' was to sense racial prejudice; to have 'eyes' for something was to approve of it. 'Bells' (sometimes elided to 'ding-dong') meant enjoyment. These are fairly straightforward, but what is one to make of 'Bing and Bob', meaning the police,[11] or 'pound cake', for wife or girlfriend? 'Ivey-divey' signified resigned acceptance of life and its inexplicable twists and turns. Then there was his penchant for bestowing names on people, many of which stuck. When the young and agreeable Harry Edison joined Basie's trumpet section, Lester immediately named him 'Sweets' because of his temperament, and it was as Harry Sweets Edison that he lived the remainder of his long life. Similarly, the short, rotund Jimmy Rushing was forever 'Mr Five By Five' (five feet tall and five feet wide). Basie was 'The Holy Main', Dickie Wells, who suffered from dyspepsia, was dubbed 'Gas Belly', and the band's road manager, whose name was Snodgrass, became 'Lady Snar'. Indeed, almost anyone was 'Lady', regardless of gender – thus 'Lady Sweets', 'Lady Webster' and, of course, 'Lady Day'.

Although Billie had left the band, Lester was still playing on her record sessions with Teddy Wilson, joining her in visits to after-hours sessions, drinking quantities of the fearsome 'top and bottom' and generally having a good time. He had now been recording regularly for just over two years, and had amassed a sizeable body of recorded work. This might be a good point at which to examine some of it.

5 jumpin' at the woodside

We must always remember that Lester Young's recording career began at the relatively advanced age of twenty-seven, when he was already at the height of his powers. When he walked into ARC's Chicago studio in November 1936 he was in possession of the equivalent of a poetic 'voice', the innumerable points of style which go to make a unique and consistent mode of expression. It was the suddenness of his arrival as much as anything that caused the initial consternation. People were simply not prepared for a voice not only so different from what they were used to, but so complete, confident and uncompromising. It is not at all surprising that his playing first found favour with young people, like the teenaged Al Cohn. They lacked preconceptions.

To begin almost at random, let us listen Lester's solo on Basie's 'Jumpin' At The Woodside', recorded on 22 August 1938. It starts with a two-bar solo break; that is to say, everything stops, including the beat laid down by the rhythm section, leaving the soloist to make an entrance. The usual position of a solo break is the two bars immediately preceding the start of a chorus. Players, especially in big bands, tend to use this brief moment in the spotlight to let off some kind of spectacular firework. Lester Young's solo break consists of a single note, the keynote, C (piano B-flat), repeated thirteen times, which should be the least spectacular move imaginable. The effect, however, is electrifying, partly because the repeated quavers (eighth-notes) continue the forward impetus of the beat through the break, but mainly because those thirteen notes, while all the same in pitch and immaculately spaced, are not in fact all the same. They differ in a way which conventional notation is incapable of showing, namely in density. Some notes are 'thick', some 'thin' and some neither one nor the other.

It is called 'false fingering', and it works like this. The saxophone has an effective range of two and a half octaves. Roughly halfway up this compass, the player, as it were, changes gear. Having raised all the keys, he depresses his left thumb, engaging a mechanism which splits the air column and starts again at the bottom. There is an overlap between these two registers, and several notes can be played with totally different fingerings, one producing an open and one a closed sound. By alternating the two, Lester was able to repeat a single note with two distinct sonorities: 'mm-aah'. With adjustments to his embouchure (the grip of the mouth on the mouthpiece) he could produce a whole series of intermediate sounds, too. He was not the first player to make use of this device, and probably got the idea originally from listening to Jimmy Dorsey, who employed it occasionally, but no one ever used it to such expressive effect. Nor is that the end of the matter. The two registers have distinct sonorities in any case, especially around the 'break', where the gear-change occurs. Academically trained players work hard to eliminate the difference, in the interests of even tone production, but Lester's early experiments had revealed that the lower, closed notes in the upper register produced a reverberant, honking sound. If we return for a moment to the first take of 'Shoe Shine Boy', we find that bars 25 to 28 of the first chorus consist entirely of the honking closed D (middle C on the piano) alternating with the bland B (piano A). The stress always falls on the D, a taut, booming note, adding significantly to the rhythmic tension of the passage.

That is a great deal of explanation for two bars of music to call forth, and the reader will be relieved to learn that not every solo is to be examined in such detail. The main point is that Lester Young's inventiveness and originality extended to the kind of lateral thinking described above. The rest of the 'Jumpin' At The Woodside' solo continues in the same vein, a combination of simplicity and vigour. The tune is in AABA form, the main A sections being harmonically a simplified variant of 'I Got Rhythm', with the bridge borrowed from 'Honeysuckle Rose'. Lester's phrases are quite sparse, with many blues inflections, and deployed with great rhythmic diversity. The whole thing flows gracefully along until, at the end of the chorus, the solo saxophone sinks back into the ensemble.

It took some time for Basie's band to settle the problem of written scores versus the 'head arrangements' evolved in rehearsal and performance, on which its whole style was based. The matter was eventually resolved as Basie's arrangers, notably Buck Clayton, Eddie Durham and Buster Harding, devised ways of formalizing head arrangements into an easy-sounding and flexible written style. A good example of this can be found in the original version of Basie's signature tune, 'One O'Clock Jump', recorded on 7 July 1937. A blues arranged by Eddie Durham, on the basis of a set of riffs assembled by Buster Smith back in Kansas City, it highlights the contrasting styles of Lester Young and Herschel Evans. Herschel takes the first twelve-bar solo, stretching and kneading the phrases in his fat, lazy, sensuous tone. This is followed by a trombone solo from George Hunt, and then comes Lester. Once again, he enters with a string of repeated notes, and once again the note is C (piano B-flat), but an octave higher than on 'Jumpin' At The Woodside'. And this time the effect is quite different. The key is E-flat (piano D-flat), so instead of being a forceful and down-to-earth tonic, the repeated notes make a floating, insubstantial sixth. The tone is pointedly delicate. Anything further removed from Herschel's directness of manner it would be hard to imagine. This was deliberate. Although they were old friends, they were temperamental opposites and kept up what anthropologists call a 'joking relationship', based on the regular exchange of genial insults. Billie Holiday, who observed it at close quarters but could never quite make it out (such antics are, after all, very much a male thing), recalled one exchange:

> Herschel: 'Why don't you buy an alto, man? You only got an alto tone!'

> Lester (tapping his forehead): 'There's things goin' on up here, man. Some of you guys are all belly.'[1]

Basie understood very well the dramatic value of the contrasting tenor styles and encouraged them to play up their mock enmity, to the extent of having them ostentatiously turn their backs on one another. Herschel Evans has often been described as a 'Coleman Hawkins man', but a few minutes' attentive listening will reveal that he was actually nothing of the sort. Although his tone was broad, and he admired Hawkins very much, he had none of Hawkins's florid harmonic vocabulary, and none of his choppy aggressiveness of phrase. Indeed, in everything but sound he was closer to Lester, which is hardly surprising, seeing that he came from Texas and, like Lester, had been brought up amid the south-western blues culture.

Despite his shyness and quiet nature, Lester Young had a well-developed sense of the dramatic. To be a member of a band like Basie's during the swing era was rather like being in a leading theatre company or high-ranking sports team. A man must be a team player and at the same time establish his own personality and style. As we have seen, Lester laid great store by making a memorable entrance, the simpler the better, and the simplest of all occurs in 'Swingin' The Blues' (16 February 1938). It consists of one note, a honking crotchet (quarter note) D (piano C), so precisely placed that, if you know the record, and thus know what is coming, it is hard not to make some kind of gesture, such as jabbing a finger, in time with it. In fact, the more one listens to this music, the closer it seems to be to both gesture and speech. It was, of course, made to be danced to, and at places such as the Savoy Ballroom, social dancing by ordinary people was taken to unprecedented heights of skill and virtuosity. In that milieu, dancing was a joint act of creativity by musicians and dancers. As Frank Manning, the great Lindy Hop dancer, later remarked: 'We had the best music all the time, and because we had the best music, we had the best dancers.'[2]

Lester Young often referred to playing a solo as 'telling a story', and there are fleeting moments in these Basie records when the back-and-forth of soloist and ensemble seems almost to become visible. The soloist tells his story – explaining, protesting, boasting, sighing – and the band becomes part chorus, part *corps de ballet*, expressing agreement, disagreement, shock, surprise or derision in both sound and mime. Jazz music at the time was blessed with such a wealth of expressive devices that instruments, brass especially, would often imitate human voices in the most uncanny way, with the words tantalizingly just out of reach. This may be too fanciful for some, like seeing pictures in the fire, but listen, say, to the opening chorus of 'Every Tub' (from the same session as 'Swingin' The Blues'). It opens with a set of breathless, tumbling pronouncements from Lester, punctuated by exclamations of surprise from the band. Then, as his story gets into its stride, the brass behind him seem to be leaning forward, repeating, 'Yes! Go On!'

Solos on these big-band records are, of necessity, brief, but there are some wonderful Lester Young moments scattered across the sides made in the first two years of the Basie band's recording career, the years of the Decca contract. In addition to those mentioned above, they include 'John's Idea', 'Out The Window', 'Time Out', 'Doggin' Around', 'Dark Rapture', 'Jive At Five' and several others.

Away from the band itself, Basie's musicians tended to stick together. Whenever the opportunity arose to put together an *ad hoc* small band for a recording session, Lester Young and Buck Clayton would be an obvious partnership, and the automatic choice of rhythm section would be the established firm of Green, Page and Jones. These were all present on 27 September 1938, for a session by a little band to be dubbed the Kansas City Six. The sixth member was Eddie Durham, who, in addition to having played trombone with Basie until recently, and proved invaluable as one of the band's leading arrangers, also played a new and virtually untried instrument, the electric guitar. Because of his exclusive contract with Decca, Basie himself was unable to take part. Very occasionally, the atmosphere of a recording session is caught on record, along with the music. Obvious examples would include Thelonious Monk's first 'Round Midnight', Charlie Parker's 'Lover Man' or Clifford Brown's Paris sessions of 1953. The five Kansas City Six pieces have that quality, in this case a palpable aura of relaxed well-being. The titles are 'Way Down Yonder In New Orleans', 'Countless Blues', 'Them There Eyes', 'I Want A Little Girl' and 'Pagin' The Devil', and there are two surviving takes of each.

The subdued dynamic level, coupled with exceptionally good recording, reveals a world of expressive detail, especially in the delicate interaction among the six players. As for the tenor saxophone solos, the first thing one notices about them is their remarkable combination of reticence and energy. Lester is obviously playing at about half the volume he used with the full Basie band, but closer to the microphone. Some of his notes are mere whispers. The free air is audible as he half-voices them, yet the improvised line is as taut as ever, firmly articulated and moving with elegance and logic. And always there is the minute adjustment of tonal weight, trimming and balancing note against note and phrase against phrase. It is in surroundings like this that the full extent of his originality can be appreciated, an originality that becomes the more astonishing as one appreciates the simplicity of the means by which it is expressed. For example, his solo in the first take of 'Way Down Yonder' looks a picture of innocence when written down, an artless stream of arpeggios and fragments of scales, almost entirely in quavers (eighth notes) and all conforming to the simple harmonic scheme of this popular song dating from 1922. And yet there is an ethereal magic about it that was quite new to jazz in 1938 and remains entrancing to this day. He achieves the effect through a combination of airy tone, tiny inflexions and a wily choice of notes. Simple they may be, but they are not obvious. Phrases tend to land not on solid common notes of a chord, such as the tonic, third of fifth, but on the less stable ground of the sixth or the ninth. Clever chromatic substitutions, which Coleman Hawkins employed in profusion, did not interest Lester Young. However, one tiny chromatic inflexion does occur in this solo. In bar 20 he plays a descending arpeggio of the chord of F7 (piano E-flat 7th) and raises the fifth by a semitone. This alteration, known as an 'augmented fifth', gives the chord a very specific flavour, an unfinished quality suggestive of emptiness, indecision or uncertainty, and Lester was very fond of it. In a buoyant solo like this it acts simply as a fleck of colour, but later he would come to employ it to powerful emotional effect.

Saxophonists in big bands were normally expected to 'double' on clarinet, and Lester plays brief clarinet passages on several Basie records, notably 'Texas Shuffle' and 'Blue And Sentimental', but the first substantial examples are to be found on these Kansas City Six recordings. It was not an instrument to which he had devoted much time and, whereas the tenor saxophone seems to be part of him, the clarinet is clearly a stranger, or at best a nodding acquaintance. As was his way with strangers, he treats the instrument with circumspection. Careful and tentative, he relies entirely on his instinct for the telling phrase and the rhythmic felicity, yet even Goodman at his most polished could not have improved on Lester Young feeling his way through 'I Want A Little Girl'. He played a metal clarinet, intended originally for robust service in military bands, and from it he produced a sound unlike anyone else's, plangent and curiously hollow. His fragile sixteen-bar solo on 'I Want A Little Girl' has been described as 'Zen-like', but it is neither mystical nor withdrawn. On the contrary, it is almost painfully candid and personal. By contrast, the final chorus of 'Way Down Yonder' finds Lester's clarinet and Buck Clayton's trumpet weaving around one another in a wonderfully loose-limbed duet improvisation that harks back to the sunny style of Lester's early heroes, Bix Beiderbecke and Frankie Trumbauer. Artie Shaw summed up a widespread view of Lester Young's relationship with the clarinet when he said, 'Lester played better clarinet than a lot of guys who played better clarinet than he did!'

Meanwhile, as John Hammond had predicted, Billie Holiday's records with small bands had been selling in decent numbers, and her recording sessions had become regular events. Sometimes the discs came out under Teddy Wilson's name, in which case Billie sang one chorus in the middle of the piece, while others were credited to 'Billie Holiday and her Orchestra'. On these she sang the opening and closing choruses, with an instrumental passage in between. Whatever the case, the general pattern of skeletal routines and short solos was the same. Between 25 January 1937 and 21 March 1940, Lester Young took part in thirteen sessions with Billie Holiday. One could pick out items from almost any one of them and find moments of beauty, but let us for the moment settle on two numbers from the session of 15 June 1937, under Billie's name. This was during her time as Basie's vocalist, to which, despite all its discomforts and hardships, she looked back fondly in her autobiography, *Lady Sings the Blues*:

> I often think about how we used to record in those days. We'd get off the bus after a five hundred-mile trip, go into the studio with no music, eat nothing but coffee and sandwiches...
>
> I'd say, 'What'll we do, two-bar or four-bar intro?' Somebody'd say, 'Make it four and a chorus – one, one and a half.'
>
> Then I'd say, 'You play behind me on the first eight, Lester.' And then Harry Edison would come in, or Buck Clayton, and take the next eight bars.

'Jo, you just brush and don't hit the cymbals too much.'

Now with all their damn preparation, complicated arrangements, you've got to kiss everyone's behind to get ten minutes to do eight sides in.[3]

The two numbers in question are 'Me, Myself And I' and 'A Sailboat In The Moonlight'. Neither is a distinguished song, the lyrics of both being quite woeful, but they serve their purpose. 'Me, Myself And I' opens with four bars from Lester, then Billie enters, with Buck Clayton tiptoeing along beside her, whispering muted comments. In the background can be heard the unmistakable mumbling sound of two players (Lester and clarinettist Edmond Hall) busking long-note harmonies in that indefinite, keeping-out-of-trouble way that prudent men adopt in such circumstances. For the next chorus Hall plays sixteen bars, Buck plays the bridge, pianist Jimmy Sherman the last eight (Teddy Wilson was away in Pittsburgh with Benny Goodman), and then comes the high point – Billie and Lester together. She may have said, 'You play behind me, Lester', but that's not what he did. The small, bright voice and the fluent saxophone conduct a conversation, half passionate, half kidding, which never palls. Neither waits for the other and then follows. They simply move as one. Apart from Armstrong in his prime, there is no more optimistic, spirit-lifting sound in jazz. 'A Sailboat In The Moonlight' contains another Billie–Lester duet chorus of comparable brilliance, plus a particularly fine eight-bar solo from him, in which he transforms the slightly pedestrian tune by introducing a series of blues inflexions. The whole thing is accomplished with casual grace, rendered more attractive by its very lack of pretentiousness.

These swing-sing records of Billie Holiday exist in great profusion. Counting only those on which Lester Young plays, they amount to forty-nine separate items, many surviving in two takes. Scattered through them are innumerable tiny moments of sheer joy. Take, for instance, Billie's entry on 'Back In Your Own Back Yard', where she places the words 'the bird' with devastating precision; or Lester's statement of the melody in 'Fooling Myself', in which he presses with infinite gentleness on the note of the tune which happens to be his beloved augmented fifth; or his tricky, unaccompanied four-bar introduction to 'If Dreams Come True'. None of these lasts more than a second or two, but each one delivers a minute shock of surprise, no matter how familiar one is with the piece.

For the second half of 1938 Basie's musicians lived a moderately settled life. What travelling they did consisted mainly of (by their standards) gentle excursions into New England and its environs, and from

July to November they were resident at the Famous Door. This accounts for the unusual amount of recorded Lester Young material dating from those months. Much of it exists in the form of broadcast recordings, either 'air checks', taken off-air from radio broadcasts, or studio recordings expressly made for radio use. One of the latter is a session recorded by Basie on 9 July 1938, for the CBS network series *America Dances*, also broadcast in Britain by the BBC. Like most such shows, it reflects the band's current nightly repertoire, and reveals two common effects of regular repetition: first, that the more often a band plays a piece, the faster the tempo becomes and, second, that even the most adventurous players end up delivering substantially the same solos after a while. Take the case of 'Every Tub', a recently recorded number which Basie was featuring at the time. The *America Dances* version goes at 268 beats per minute, as compared with the original record's 232, while Lester, Herschel and Harry Edison play virtually identical solos to those they play on the original. On the other hand, Lester produces an exquisitely poised and fresh-sounding thirty-two bars on 'Flat Foot Floogie', the novelty hit of the day.

The year ended with another Carnegie Hall concert, staged on 23 December by John Hammond, under the vaguely pedagogic title *From Spirituals to Swing*. Its intention was to illustrate the development of jazz, with the Basie band, plus various guests, as the 'swing' element in the programme. The surviving, somewhat sketchy, recording features a reunion between Basie and Hot Lips Page. One of the two numbers that Page plays with the band, 'Rhythm Man', goes at a fierce tempo but Lester skips through sixteen bars with complete aplomb, a model of cool relaxation.

The last sessions under Basie's Decca contract were recorded in a bunch in January and February 1939. The three years were not quite up, and instead of making the stipulated seventy-two sides they finally managed sixty-three, of which ten were by Basie and the rhythm section alone. Dave Kapp turned up backstage at the Apollo Theatre, bearing a thousand dollars in cash as an inducement to Basie to sign up again. Basie turned him down, although he needed the money, and Kapp, realizing the game was up, let him go. As luck would have it, that final group of Decca sessions produced two miniature Lester Young masterpieces. The first, on 2 February, was 'You Can Depend On Me', a song with music by Earl Hines and lyric by Charlie Carpenter, who was to become Lester's personal manager in later years. The band consists only of Lester, trumpeter and newcomer Shad Collins, Basie and the rhythm section, plus Jimmy Rushing. As a three-minute jazz performance it's just about perfect, with

Rushing singing the opening chorus, followed by solos from Lester and Shad, and finishing with a set of four-bar exchanges by trumpet, piano and saxophone. Lester's solo is an airy melody, so shapely and enticing that not only has it been used as a theme on its own account by players of subsequent generations, it also had words set to it by Jon Hendricks, for a version recorded by the vocal group Manhattan Transfer in 1975. For some reason, this was the only number recorded at the session, which is a matter of great regret. The other piece, recorded two days later, is 'Jive At Five'. Once again, only part of the band is involved – the trumpet section and rhythm section plus Dickie Wells, baritone saxophonist Jack Washington and Lester. The ensemble is feather-light, with Wells adding a growling commentary. Lester's solo floats blithely through and above the accompaniment, sounding so free that, although his line follows the descending chromatic chords in the sequence, the notes seem to fit almost by accident.

The band resumed touring after the Famous Door residency came to an end, and it was playing at the Crystal Ballroom in Hertford, Connecticut when Herschel Evans collapsed on stage from a heart attack. He had been feeling unwell for some weeks and had missed the band's final Decca recording session, but had been determined to make the tour. His big feature number, 'Blue And Sentimental', was getting a lot of radio exposure and he was looking forward to his nightly moment in the spotlight. He died in hospital on 9 February 1939. The effect on Lester was devastating. He and Herschel had been friends and colleagues since Kansas City days. Rather like an old married couple, they had argued and bickered endlessly, but beneath it all they had been very close. Lester's first impulse was to do what he had always done when faced with an unpleasant situation. He tried to run away. Jack Washington spent half his time on stage grabbing Lester and holding him down in his chair. The panic gradually subsided, but Lester's grief remained and he would often speak fondly of Herschel.

After a period in which Herschel's place was filled by a series of temporary substitutes, Basie settled on Buddy Tate, another Texan, as a permanent replacement. It happened when the band passed through Kansas City on 2 March 1939. Lester met Tate and tipped him off. 'There's a lot of ladies want the engagement – Lady Berry, Lady Webster [but] if you're playing like you did the last time I heard you, it'll be your engagement.'[4] Tate clinched the matter himself that night, by playing 'Blue And Sentimental', Herschel's feature, to perfection. The band returned to New York shortly afterwards, and as he got off the train Tate found himself at a loss:

I'm standing at Grand Central Station, and I know I looked terrible. I know you could see country written all over me... I didn't know where to go. I looked around and there was nobody there, and Prez was standing in the corner... He says, 'You have to forgive the ladies. They haven't seen their madam queens and everybody's lonely. So that's why they leave you. They mean well.' So he carried me on up to the Woodside.[5]

The Woodside (of 'Jumpin' At The Woodside' fame) was a Harlem hotel-cum-rooming house where most of the musicians, including Lester Young and Mary Dale, lived when in New York. To accommodate couples, it had some small apartments with cooking facilities and there was a very large basement containing a piano, where rehearsals could take place.

Basie was now free to sign the recording contract that John Hammond had intended for him all along. The American Record Corporation had been taken over by CBS/Columbia, and it was for Columbia's Vocalion label that Basie now began recording on 13 February 1939. It was not a comfortable start. Herschel's replacement had not then been decided, so Basie elected to record with a reduced band, an octet to be dubbed 'Basie's Bad Boys'. They had been playing in Chicago the previous night and the session was held at the old ARC studios there. The heating had broken down, and Chicago in February is bitterly cold, so the musicians were forced to play in their overcoats. They recorded four numbers under these conditions, only to discover that the equipment had been malfunctioning. Accordingly, the material was shelved. It lay undisturbed for thirteen years before being unearthed, polished up by post-war technology and released in 1952. Subsequent digital transfers have improved the sound quality even further. With the cavernous acoustics of a big, cold studio, the results lack the intimacy and definition of the Kansas City Six sides, but they are remarkably good nonetheless. Lester plays clarinet on the opening number, 'I Ain't Got Nobody', taking the lead after Basie's opening chorus, switches to tenor during Buck Clayton's trumpet solo and follows with a beautifully shaped chorus, before switching quickly back to clarinet for the final ensemble. His clarinet tone sounds a little acrid on this session (probably the result of the recording problems), but in all other respects it is vintage Lester Young. There happened to be an organ in the studio and Basie, like his mentor Fats Waller, could never resist climbing aboard one of those. Accordingly, for the next two pieces, 'Goin' To Chicago Blues' and 'Live And Love Tonight', he plays organ instead of piano. Electric organs were at an early stage of development in 1939, and lacked the sharpness and punch which were to make the Hammond organ a popular jazz instrument in the 1960s. Basie's organ playing is something of an acquired taste, but he uses its effects sparingly, and his backing to Lester on 'Live And Love Tonight' is exquisitely apt. Lester's solo on the final number, 'Love Me Or Leave Me', has an authentic springiness that recalls his debut 'Shoe Shine Boy', although its impact is blunted by the fact that his microphone seems not to be working and his sound comes from afar, surrounded by echo.

Figure 5. 1939/40. Three of Basie's star soloists – Harry 'Sweets' Edison, Buddy Tate and Lester Young. Location and exact date unknown. (Peter Vacher collection)

Herschel's death, the arrival of Buddy Tate and the change of record label mark a new chapter in the Basie band's history. It now numbered fifteen players and would soon be expanded to sixteen. The old, organic Kansas City head-arrangement approach, so dear to Basie's heart, was gradually being displaced by sharper and more colourful orchestrations. Public taste demanded it. But the change was gradual and the recordings made over the remainder of 1939 and 1940 catch the band's music at a fine point of balance between the two. In fact, 'Taxi War Dance', the first full-band recording under the new contract to feature Lester significantly, is an archetypal solos-and-riffs head arrangement. The title is a three-way pun: 'taxi dance' (as in ten-cents-a-dance ballrooms where you paid a partner to dance with you), 'taxi war' (a cab drivers' dispute then raging in New York), and 'war dance' (as in Indian war dance). Lester's main solo comes at the very beginning. Opening with a twisted quotation from 'Ol' Man River', he jumps in as though propelled by powerful elastic. The harmonic sequence is, in effect, a truncated version of the ballad 'Willow Weep For Me'. The way he flips lightly through the chord changes, touching each one deftly while carving an elegant and energetic line, puts one in mind of a gymnast or ballet dancer. He arrives at the final cadence at the last possible moment, landing with a negligent little bounce. No one else could have done it because no one else's mind worked that way. The thought and its expression are one and instantaneous, and that is what makes jazz unique in Western music. This piece also contains some four-bar solo fragments by Buddy Tate, which illustrate vividly the difference in their sounds, and, towards the end, a bravura demonstration of false fingering by Lester. He chafed increasingly at the constrictions of big-band playing, but it is the very constriction which gives these solos their unique force, a sense of endless possibilities briefly glimpsed.

Some of the best work Lester Young ever recorded is to be heard on these 1939–40 Columbia tracks. Take, for instance, 'Twelfth Street Rag', recorded in April 1939. An unpromising choice of tune, you might think, especially during the mildly comic business between Basie and Jo Jones in the opening chorus. But then comes a wonderfully light and twinkling second Basie chorus, followed by a completely unexpected change of key, from C to E-flat, and Lester bursts forth with two spectacular choruses. His mastery of rhythm is particularly impressive here, as he drops lazy, lagging phrases into an energetic and mobile improvised line, and there is a marvellous variety of tone, including a brief, machine-gun burst of false fingering in the second chorus. As always, Basie's accompaniment is discreet but brilliantly alert, following every move and nuance. In view of all this we can forgive the scrambled and perfunctory ending of the piece.

'Clap Hands, Here Comes Charlie!', recorded in August 1939, seems an even more unlikely choice than 'Twelfth Street Rag', and it moves at an unfeasibly fast 288 beats a minute, yet Lester's solo is a model of poise, as well as being a technical *tour de force*. Other band pieces from this period with notable Lester Young solos include 'Pound Cake', 'I Never Knew', 'Broadway', 'Easy Does It' and 'Louisiana', but special mention must be made of Lester's own composition, 'Tickle Toe'. Although he is credited as co-writer of several Basie numbers, having contributed ideas, riffs and so on to numerous head arrangements, this quite elaborate minor-key theme, orchestrated by Andy Gibson, was entirely his. His thirty-two-bar solo immediately follows the opening theme and grows so naturally and symmetrically out of it that they form a single entity. The theme, when it returns towards the end, is slightly altered – the alteration taking in an exact quotation from Bix Beiderbecke's solo on 'When?', recorded with

Paul Whiteman's orchestra in 1928. Lester's legendary musical memory was clearly still in full working order. It turned out, in later years, that 'Tickle Toe' was one of the pieces which Lester's acolytes of the Al Cohn generation strove to master, and sometimes played, and even recorded, as adult musicians in the 1950s and beyond. Thus, Bix's happy moment of invention was passed on down the decades.

Figure 6. 1940. Count Basie and his Orchestra, recording at Columbia Studios, New York. Dated 'March 1940', this could well be 19 March session, at which they recorded the glorious 'Tickle Toe'. (Frank Driggs collection)

The intimate circumstances of the Kansas City Six sessions were reproduced on an official Basie recording in September 1939, when a small group from the orchestra recorded two titles under the name of the Kansas City Seven. This time the full Basie rhythm section was in attendance, along with Lester, Buck Clayton and Dickie Wells. The first number, which came out under the title 'Dickie's Dream', was originally called 'Conversation Piece', which would have been an appropriate title, because that's what it sounds like, especially between Lester and Dickie Wells, whose solos seem, in some magical way, to be expressing two sides of the same argument – Wells with his canny, dry humour and Lester at his most mercurial. When Wells takes over at the end of Lester's solo, he starts by repeating Lester's final three notes, thus emphasizing the continuity of the discourse. Jazz tunes with the word 'Dream' in the title are almost always in a minor key, as this is, and usually feature the chord of the minor sixth (a minor triad with an added major sixth). This ambiguous chord does suggest a mildly dreamlike atmosphere, and Lester deploys the sixth to great effect in his solo. The other number recorded from this session is 'Lester Leaps In', a riff on 'I Got Rhythm' which came to be regarded as Lester's signature tune. His solo here is noteworthy for two reasons – first because it is formidably well constructed, with several cunningly off-centre phrases, and second because Basie mistakenly comes in at the start of Lester's second chorus, causing a major collision. Lester carries doggedly on while Basie stops to get his bearings, and they're back on track eight bars later. A second take was recorded but Lester's solo was not so good, so the first was released, collision included.

Like all professional musicians, Lester Young occasionally found himself in some peculiar situations. One of these was a recording session on 26 June 1939, under the leadership of Glenn Hardman, an organist in possession either of a majestically dead-pan sense of humour or misplaced self-confidence of mind-boggling proportions. The electric organ, as mentioned earlier, was a pretty unwieldy item in those days. Basie could just about make it swing, but even he didn't tempt providence by dispensing with the bass player and relying on his own efforts with the bass-pedals. This, plus Hardman's enthusiastic use of the instrument's various stops and effects, imparts an air of the fairground to all six numbers recorded that day. Apart from Lester, the others present were Freddie Green, Jo Jones, and trumpeter Lee Castle, a member of Tommy Dorsey's band at the time. They clearly took the job seriously, and in fact play very well, especially Lester, who turns in some lovely clarinet on 'Who?', but Hardman's playing is so gloopy, and some of his ideas so endearingly daft (like, for instance, attaching a skirling Scottish introduction to the front of 'Jazz Me Blues'), that one can easily imagine the looks that passed among them as the session proceeded.

Meanwhile, Billie Holiday's fame had been growing. Her debut at the prestigious new club, 'Café Society', in Greenwich Village had attracted a following among the liberal intelligentsia. Her recording sessions were now not quite the cut-price affairs they had been, which meant that 'Billie Holiday and her Orchestra' no longer consisted of half a dozen good players who happened to be free on a given day. Bigger bands meant written arrangements and an end to the cosy informality of earlier times. Lester did take part in some of these later sessions, and can be heard playing several half-chorus solos – for instance on 'The Man I Love' and 'You're A Lucky Guy', from December 1939, and 'I'm Pulling Through' and 'Laughing At Life', from June 1940. From this latter session comes a version of 'Time On My Hands', where he plays alongside Billie, but his sound is thrust so far into the background that it is difficult to make out what he's doing.

In the summer of 1939, with a European war looming, Coleman Hawkins finally returned home. One of the first things he did was to record 'Body And Soul', a monumentally impressive and ornate improvisation on Johnny Green's ballad, in which the original melody scarcely dares peep out. To everyone's surprise, including Hawkins's, the record scored a mammoth jukebox hit, and was universally hailed as a masterpiece. He and Lester soon faced each other at a number of jam sessions, notably one held at Puss Johnson's Tavern in Harlem, which was reported in *Down Beat*. Opinions were divided about who came off best, although the report suggested it was Hawkins. This drew a furious letter from Billie, who had been present, asserting that Prez had 'cut the Hawk' and that 'most everyone there who saw them tangle agreed on that'.[6] The fact was that the two were so different in every way – harmonically, rhythmically and temperamentally – that no sensible qualitative comparisons could be made, but Hawkins's return did present Lester with a powerful rival in the affections of jazz lovers.

Another arrival in the latter part of 1939 was the guitarist Charlie Christian. Seven years younger than Lester, he came from a very similar background. He had been born in Dallas, Texas, and raised in Oklahoma City. His father, who was blind, led a family string band of strolling players. Christian had attended the same school as the future novelist Ralph Ellison, the one who so vividly recalled hearing Lester jamming in an Oklahoma City shoeshine parlour. The impressionable teenaged Christian is likely to have heard him, too. He certainly knew about Lester, because every musician in the south-west did. Christian began experimenting with electric amplification for the guitar, in order to be able to play single-line solos, like a saxophone. The guitarist Mary Osborne recalled standing outside a cabaret in Bismarck, North Dakota, in about 1934, and hearing what she thought was a tenor saxophone being played into a microphone. On going inside, she discovered it was Charlie Christian, playing a guitar with a microphone attached to it. So when, finally, the first reliable, commercially produced electric guitar came onto the market, in 1937, Charlie Christian was ready and waiting with a fully developed technique and vocabulary for it. Inevitably, it was John Hammond who discovered him and got him into Benny Goodman's band.

Charlie Christian's guitar and Lester Young's tenor saxophone could sound quite uncannily alike, and they played with the same kind of relaxed, blues-inflected fluency. They played together in jam sessions at Minton's Playhouse in Harlem and briefly at the second *From Spirituals to Swing* concert at Carnegie Hall on Christmas Eve 1939. Christian was a member, along with vibraphonist Lionel Hampton, of Goodman's sextet, which appeared as a special feature with his big band. After a while, Basie himself began making guest appearances, too, and also recording with the sextet. Then Lionel Hampton left, to form his own band, and Goodman had the idea of recasting the sextet as a seven-piece ('Benny Goodman *and* his Sextet'), along the lines of the Kansas City Seven. And who better for the other two front-line members than Lester Young and Buck Clayton? Thus is was that, on 28 October 1940, Lester, Buck, Charlie Christian, Goodman, Basie, Jo Jones and Goodman's bassist, Artie Bernstein, met in a New York studio to make a trial recording.

The five resulting numbers contain some of Lester's most delicate playing in the 'chamber jazz' context. On all five numbers, especially 'Ad Lib Blues' and two versions of the same minor-key theme, 'Lester's Dream' and 'Charlie's Dream', he plays with a kind of subdued excitement. The blues, in particular, is quite magnificent, as he uncoils great, serpentine loops of melody over the first four bars of each chorus. And the obvious empathy between Lester and Charlie stands out a mile. They speak the same language and their minds work in a similar way. Listening to them together, they could be brothers. Of all the might-have-beens in jazz, the prospect of a long and fruitful association between Lester Young and Charlie Christian is one of the most poignant. The sextet idea did finally take off, but without Lester or Buck, and Charlie died of TB less than two years later, at the age of twenty-two.

6 just jivin' around

On 1 January 1941, *Down Beat* magazine carried the following news item:

> Lester Young and Count Basie, friends and co-workers for the past five years in Basie's band, parted two weeks ago. The split came as a terrific surprise to followers of Basie and the band. Basie said he would not comment. Young...likewise refused to discuss the change and said he wasn't sure what he would do... Les, who failed to show up for a record date on Friday 13th [December], said 'Go 'way and lemme sleep – a man's got no business makin' music on Friday the 13th'.

The news came from out of the blue. No one believed the Friday 13th story, although Lester apparently did say something of the sort, in order to get rid of the reporter, but neither could anyone imagine what had caused the split. One thing is certain: everybody was remarkably tight-lipped, both at the time and subsequently. Basie steered benignly away from the subject whenever it hove into view, and when Lester was asked the straight question, 'Why did you leave Count Basie in 1940?' he replied, 'That's some deep question you're asking me now. Skip that one, but I sure could tell you, but it wouldn't be sporting. I still have nice eyes... The thing is still cool with me because I don't bother nobody...' etc., etc.[1]

The next issue of the two-weekly *Down Beat* announced: 'Don Byas will probably inherit Lester Young's tenor chair. Basie has been using several subs since Young was fired.' This was followed in the 1st March issue by a letter in the 'Chords and Dischords' section of the paper: 'To the Editors – May I correct Mr Ed Flynn, who wrote in the Jan 15 "Down Beat" that Lester Young (formerly of Count Basie's orchestra) was fired. My husband was not fired. He quit for reasons of his own. I will appreciate your making this clear. Mrs Lester (Mary) Young.' Presumably, the old horror of being seen as an outcast had arisen again; Lester had brooded over the report and become so agitated that Mary had written to the paper in an effort to relieve the tension at home.

But what was it all about? What really happened? By examining circumstances in and around the Basie band in late 1940, together with what we know of Lester's personality, it is possible to make a few educated guesses. In the first place, the band was sailing through some choppy water at the time. Willard Alexander, who had diligently watched over Basie's career since 1936, had left MCA and joined the rival William Morris agency. Without his guiding presence, MCA were reportedly not taking proper care of the band's interests, sending it on strings of one-nighters, up to 500 miles apart, failing to book it into locations with radio links, leaving long, unprofitable gaps in the diary and being generally negligent. When work was sparse, Basie would take himself off to appear as featured guest artist with Benny Goodman, which did little for the morale of the others. There were even rumours that the band might break up. In these unstable circumstances the normally happy atmosphere among the musicians became clouded by bickering and petty disputes. For reasons which remain unclear, the trumpeter Shad Collins, a particular friend of Lester's, left the band, to be replaced by high-note specialist Al Killian.

This was the moment when Lester chose to ask for a pay rise. Rates of pay for big-band musicians were going up, especially for featured soloists, and it was a perfectly reasonable request. But the management problems meant that the band wasn't making as much money as it should have been. It seems that Basie consulted John Hammond about Lester's request, and Hammond advised him that he really couldn't afford to give pay rises at the moment. This got back to Lester, who took it personally and conceived an enduring hostility towards Hammond.

Lester was finding the routine of playing in a saxophone section increasingly irksome. The arrangements, as we have seen, were becoming more formal and elaborate (which may explain the departure of Shad Collins, to make way for Al Killian), and that meant fewer opportunities for the creative section work involved in head arrangements. At the same time, there was a fair amount of movement going on in the band business, with soloists leaving to form their own bands, the most recent example being Lionel Hampton's split from Goodman. We can be pretty certain that people had been asking Lester whether he was thinking of making a similar move.

Put all that together – MCA's mismanagement, the refusal of a pay rise, the unsatisfying section work, the departure of Shad Collins, the generally disgruntled atmosphere, the example of Hampton and others – add to this the reappearance of Hawkins and his success with 'Body And Soul', and you have an almost irresistible pressure to make some kind of move. The flaw lay in those few words in the first *Down Beat* report: 'Young...said he wasn't sure what he would do'. Lester had made no preparation for the move and had no one to advise him on what to do next. The only person with any kind of idea was John Hammond, who suggested an alliance in a joint venture with Billie Holiday. Lester turned this down out of hand, mainly, one suspects, because it came from Hammond.

Successful bandleaders were not, on the whole, sensitive or retiring souls. If the words of their former employees are anything to go by, the spectrum of their characters covered martinets, sadists, cold-fish and all-round sons-of-bitches. A few were recognizable as human beings; Harry James and Woody Herman being two. Basie was in a class of his own. From about the age of thirty he had been rehearsing the part of genial, absent-minded old buffer. He played it to perfection, but was canny and always got his own way. He also relied on other people to do the dirty work. Lester Young was shy, sweet-natured, impractical and apt to run away at the first sign of trouble or conflict. He was in his element on the back seat of a tour bus, commenting on the passing scene in his private language, giving his friends funny names, smoking pot, shooting craps and losing money. The neutral observer would readily conclude that here was not one of nature's bandleaders.

Figure 7. 1940 (December). Lester had just left Basie and was playing in jam sessions around New York City while assembling his own band. This was taken on a Monday night at the Village Vanguard. (Charles Peterson, courtesy of Don Peterson)

Looking back, Lester may well have recalled his first dramatic move, on the day when he stood up to his father and left the family band. That had been a liberating experience. He had fallen on his feet. With the exception of the Henderson episode, he had managed pretty well since, and was now the star of a world-famous band. Everything would work out fine. All he had to do was get his own little band together, rehearse it, fix up a resident gig to get it established and take off from there. Since he had kept up the practice of playing in jam sessions whenever possible, he knew dozens, possibly even hundreds, of musicians and their capabilities, so choosing the band posed no problem. For his front-line partner he hired his pal, trumpeter Shad Collins. He loved the new sound of the electric guitar, as introduced by Charlie Christian, and got one of Christian's closest disciples, John Collins (no relation to Shad), for that place. At jam sessions at Minton's Playhouse in Harlem he found bassist Nick Fenton and drummer Harold 'Doc' West. He did not originally intend to have a piano in the band, but he heard a young pianist named Clyde Hart and added him to the strength.

They rehearsed in the basement at the Woodside and some isolated gigs came along during the first few weeks. One of these, at the Manhattan Center, was broadcast and two pieces survive. The date is unknown, but it was probably quite early, before Clyde Hart joined, because there is no piano present. The two numbers are 'Tickle Toe' and 'Taxi War Dance', both recent hits with Basie. Lester may have been looking for some format that broke with the traditional theme-solos-theme shape of small-band jazz, because each one starts with solos and concludes with band riffs. On the other hand, this may have been at the very beginning of the band's existence, before they had learned the tunes properly. This would explain why Lester's wonderful 'Tickle Toe' melody does not appear at all, the piece finishing with a couple of riff choruses. In fact, the only thing that makes it recognizable as 'Tickle Toe' is the chord sequence, although Lester opens his solo with a break virtually identical with the one he plays on the Basie record. It is the same story with 'Taxi War Dance', identifiable only by its chord sequence, although 'Taxi War Dance' didn't really have a theme in the first place, the Basie original being a confection of riffs and solos. Altogether, the band sounds pretty rough and ready, although the solos are fine. Lester himself sounds smooth and elegant, exactly as he does on the Kansas City Seven records.

A residency was duly booked at a well-known club, Kelly's Stable, which had recently relocated to 137 West 52nd Street. It was a good move, since Lester's name would be replacing that of Coleman Hawkins on the marquee. A press agent would have made good use of the 'challenger succeeds reigning champion' angle here, but Lester didn't have a press agent and nobody else seems to have thought of it. The band opened on 27 February, sharing the bill with singer-pianist Una Mae Carlisle, and seemed to be settling in well. Less than three weeks later, everything fell apart. According to John Collins: 'The bandstand was right by the aisle that led to the kitchen, which meant that the waiters had to come and go right by the bandstand all night long... Prez stepped off the bandstand and one of the waiters bumped right into him.'[2] There was a brisk exchange of words and Prez, as anyone who knew him could have predicted, simply walked out. What was said, we don't know. Dark rumours of racial insult arose, but it was all speculation. Lester later claimed that the owner, Ralph Watkins, was a 'crow' (racist), but at this distance in time that is impossible to prove or disprove. It has been said that proprietors of jazz clubs in New York preferred to hire waiters with no interest in music, thereby ensuring that they paid attention to the job in hand, and there were some feisty characters among them.

Figure 8. 1941. The ill-fated Lester Young band at Kelly's Stable, with (l to r): Harold 'Doc' West (drums), Shad Collins (trumpet), Lester, Nick Fenton (bass), Clyde Hart (piano), John Collins (guitar). (Frank Driggs collection)

So that was the end of that. They were out of a job, with no management, no recording contract and no prospects of further employment. There exists, however, one curious memento of the full, short-lived Lester Young band. Una Mae Carlisle, who shared the bill with them at Kelly's Stable, did have a recording contract with RCA Victor. She liked and admired Lester and the rest of the band and booked them to accompany her at a recording session on 10 February. A discovery and protégée of Fats Waller, Una Mae had packed a lot into her twenty-five years. She had travelled to Britain with the show *Blackbirds of 1936* and stayed on, performing first in London, then in Paris and finally in Berlin, where she was appearing when war was declared. It is ironic that this talented and engaging artist should now be remembered almost solely for two recorded numbers on which Lester Young takes solos – 'Beautiful Eyes' and the bizarre 'Blitzkrieg Baby (You Can't Bomb Me)'. The band is obviously capable of far more than it is asked to do, and Lester holds back during his brief solos.

In New York City, Lester Young could never be said to be at a loose end. So long as there were jam sessions to play at, he was busy. Monday nights were usually passed at the Village Vanguard; others were often spent up in Harlem, at Monroe's Uptown House or at Minton's, where Charlie Christian turned up as often as he could (the management even bought a guitar amplifier, to save him the trouble of dragging his own along), and the very first stirrings of the new jazz, soon to be known as 'bebop', were taking place. Some established swing players had difficulty understanding what was going on, and they got no help from the young experimenters, who did all they could to frighten them off, but, by all accounts, Prez managed to fit in without changing his approach in the least. His superb ear allowed him to glide blithely through the tough, impacted harmonies. There were also casual gigs, and even a few recording sessions. The very last of Billie Holiday's Columbia sessions on which he played took place on 21 March. The eight-piece band was led by Eddie Heywood and the music was far more tightly arranged than in the early days. Lester, who managed to get Shad and John Collins onto the session with him, plays a gorgeous eight bars in 'All Of Me'. It may be the close-miked recording, but there is a slight huskiness in his tone here that is quite new. There's just a hint of it, too, in the product of the next session, by Sammy Price and his Texas Bluesicians, dating from 3 April, although the recording is not as sharp. Lester plays solos on three of the four numbers, including some masterly opening breaks (à la 'Every Tub') and a fine chorus on 'Just Jivin' Around'.

Even though the faithful Shad Collins was still on hand, there seemed no prospect of reviving the band, and jam sessions and casual gigs were getting him nowhere. He couldn't go back to Basie, even though the MCA business had now been settled; John Hammond was *persona non grata*, so he couldn't go to him for help; Goodman had set up his sextet by now, with Georgie Auld in the place Lester might have taken. Money was short. Where could he turn? He called his younger brother, Lee, in Los Angeles for help. Lee was now a successful musician and bandleader. He had played drums with Fats Waller, Les Hite and briefly with the young Nat King Cole and had worked at both Paramount and MGM studios in Hollywood. He had been both singer and drummer with Lionel Hampton's first big band and was now leading his own quintet, the Esquires of Rhythm, at the Club Capri in Los Angeles. He was smart, personable and business-minded. He played golf and did work for charity. In short, he was a credit to his father, and everything that Lester was not. Some years earlier, while visiting Los Angeles, John Hammond had called on Billy Young and told him how much he admired his son.

> 'Which one?' Billy asked.
>
> 'Why, Lester,' Hammond replied.
>
> 'Lester! Oh, no. The great person in my family is Lee.'
>
> 'I got the impression', Hammond later remarked, 'that he thought Lester was practically a madman.'[3]

That is probably putting it a bit too strongly, but puzzled exasperation there certainly was, and Billy Young was not a man to disguise his opinions. Lester would have been well aware that his father spoke of him in mildly contemptuous terms and compared him unfavourably with his younger brother. It cannot have been easy for him, asking Lee for help, but Lee readily offered him a place in the Esquires of Rhythm. Lester and Mary duly left for California in May 1941.

The Esquires of Rhythm already had an excellent tenor saxophonist in Bumps Myers, who was popular with audiences and highly regarded by other musicians. Lee had no intention of firing Bumps in order to make way for Lester, and arranged to enlarge the band from a five to a six-piece. But this couldn't happen immediately. Because Lester would be taking up a full-time job, he would have to transfer his union membership from the New York local of the American Federation of Musicians (AFM) to the LA branch. Before he could do this he would have to wait out a validation period of six weeks, during which he would be allowed to appear only as a 'guest artist', playing three numbers per set, standing on the dance floor in front of the band. Live entertainment is almost always hedged with bizarre and pointless regulations. Usually these are devised by legislators, but sometimes, as in this case, they are imposed by representatives of the performers themselves.

When Lester finally joined the band on stage, its sound, according to Lee Young, was very impressive. They built up a splendid book of arrangements, including several by Duke Ellington's co-composer, Billy Strayhorn, who was in town with Ellington, working on their musical, *Jump For Joy*. In one respect at least Lee's band was ahead of its time, in that it employed the electric guitar as a front-line instrument, playing single-note lines along with the trumpet and two saxophones. By the end of the year the band's name had changed from the 'Esquires of Rhythm' to 'Lee and Lester Young's Orchestra'. The Club Capri was owned by Billy Berg, a man who seems to have been one of those rare creatures, a genuinely music-loving nightclub proprietor. He certainly knew how to make the most of the available talent. Lee and Lester were joined by the guitar-and-bass duo known as 'Slim and Slam' – Slim Gaillard and Slam Stewart. Slim's main talent was for inventing and singing crazy-hip novelty numbers, such as his big hit, 'Flat-Foot Floogie'. Since he wielded a line in verbal innovation as extreme as Lester's, the bandstand at the Capri must sometimes have resembled a latter-day Tower of Babel. The club had a radio link to station KHJ, part of the Mutual network, and there were twice-weekly broadcasts. The few fragments which survive reveal a mature and swinging band. One un-named piece, which employs the Goodman riff known as 'Benny's Bugle' over the chords of 'Sweethearts On Parade', features Lester in marvellously buoyant form, incisive yet light as a feather.

In some respects, Lester's move to LA was a homecoming. His father and stepmother had been living there for years, as had Lee and his sister, Irma, along with numerous cousins, nephews and nieces, to whom he was universally known as 'Uncle Bubba'. Billy Young now worked part-time for the local 'coloured' branch of the AFM. In Los Angeles, as in many parts of the US, the union was still segregated into black and white sections. Indeed, LA was notorious for its racial prejudice, especially those parts of the city where the black population was expanding. Devotees of Raymond Chandler will recall the opening pages of *Farewell My Lovely* (1940), in which Moose Malloy goes seeking his old flame, Velma, on 'one of the mixed blocks over on Central Avenue that are not yet all negro'. Billy Young and family lived at 1706 Central Avenue. Life was especially difficult for racially mixed couples, like Lester and Mary. Even walking down the street together could be an ordeal. The relationship came under increasing strain. They parted for a while and Mary returned to New York. Following the break, Lester took up with a woman remembered only as Teddy, whom he called 'Teddy Bear'. This relation-ship lasted until his return to New York, and a temporary reunion with Mary, in August 1942.

On a night towards the end of April 1942, the band turned up for work at the Capri as usual, only to discover that Billy Berg's licence had been revoked, presumably for some obscure infringement, and they were all out of a job. It took him only a week to find new premises, at the corner of Beverly Boulevard and Fairfax Avenue in Hollywood, and set up under a new name, the Trouville Club. The move turned out well. This was Hollywood's Golden Age, and the club attracted crowds of free-spending patrons, including such movie stars at Bette Davis, Clark Gable, Lana Turner and Orson Welles. It was also the first year of America's involvement in World War II, with thousands of troops passing through west-coast ports *en route* to the Pacific conflict.

The club's first big guest attraction was Billie Holiday, who appeared there nightly during June and July. Lester's joy at the reunion was plain to everyone. Pianist Jimmy Rowles was fascinated by their relationship:

> You put the two of them together, it's pretty wild. They'd meet and stop, and he'd say, 'How are you, Miss Lady Day, Lady Day?' and he'd give her a silly look. She'd be saying 'Hey, you motherfucker!' And she'd back off, and they'd come together, and she'd be hugging him...[or] they'd just touch, like goldfish or something. Like accidental joy. And she was happy all the time.[4]

In fact, everyone seems to have been quite happy. By all accounts, the settled life in LA agreed with Lester. He was co-leader of the band, with Lee taking care of the business side, and the Trouville was a pleasant and amusing place in which to play, with reasonable working hours and good companions on hand. The years 1941–42 have often been represented as 'wilderness years' for Lester Young, but this is probably because the brothers' band never made any formal recordings and nothing very dramatic seems to have happened. In jazz terms, the west coast was still something of a backwater, but that was about to change, and some of the first stirrings actually occurred at the Trouville. A young jazz fan, Norman Granz, was a regular visitor to the club. He was working as a junior film editor at MGM studios while waiting to be drafted. Granz was keen to become involved in promoting his favourite musicians, and also in undermining the widespread culture of racial discrimination, about which he felt very strongly. He conceived the idea of setting up jam sessions and charging the public admission to attend. He discussed the matter with Billy Berg, who agreed to let him hire the Trouville on Sunday afternoons, when the place would otherwise have been closed.

The events attracted a very different crowd from the night-time clientele – college students, servicemen, impecunious jazz lovers of all kinds – and the focus was purely on music, not drinking or dancing. Despite the jam-session format, he ensured that the musicians were properly booked and paid, and insisted that there should be no racial discrimination, either overt or hidden.

At first, the musicians were not so much suspicious as puzzled. 'He was a real Joe College type', Lee Young recalled, 'with the brown-and-white shoes, the open collar, the sweater and general Sloppy Joe style. He was just a guy that was always around, and at first we wondered what he did for a living. He was a lone wolf.' But they soon became firm friends. 'Before long, I'd be going over to his side of town and he'd be visiting mine, and we'd be playing tennis.'[5] In 1942 Los Angeles this was very unusual. The pianist at some of those first Trouville jam sessions was Nat King Cole, who also became a close friend. 'Even in those days he wouldn't knuckle down to anybody', Cole remarked. 'A lot of people disliked him, but I understood his attitude.'[6]

It was Granz who set up and produced Lester's next recording, a trio session with Nat Cole and bassist Red Callender, on 15 July 1942. Despite the fact that he had been recording since 1936, this is the first time that he is heard in a purely solo role. Not only was this new to Lester Young, the whole idea of soloist-with-rhythm was fairly new in jazz. In view of the fact that it was soon to become a dominant form, this may come as a surprise, but earlier instances of the format are few and far between, and confined mainly to clarinettists (Johnny Dodds with Jimmy Blythe's Washboard Ragamuffins, Barney Bigard with Jelly Roll Morton, etc.). Even Hawkins's celebrated 'Body And Soul' has subdued band chords at various points. The format, which Stan Getz once described as 'the jazz equivalent of the string quartet',[7] puts the soloist in charge of the performance, free to decide matters such as introduction, tempo, routine, coda, and so on. It is the perfect medium to convey a soloist's full personality, and in the years since 1942 has produced some of the greatest glories of the jazz art.

Because we have not heard Lester in this context before, we cannot be sure that the way he plays on these four pieces with Nat Cole and Red Callender is new, but it certainly sounds different. His tone is heavier and has a looser texture, and in place of the leaping boldness of 'Shoe Shine Boy' or the soft tenderness of 'I Want A Little Girl', there is a sidelong, laconic quality about his phrasing. The four numbers are 'Indiana', 'I Can't Get Started', 'Tea For Two' and, interestingly, 'Body And Soul'. They mark the beginning of his transition into a different kind of artist, a change described by Gunther Schuller as 'from a compelling blues- and riff-oriented swinger, playing mostly for dances, into a romantic ballad player, appearing as a soloist at clubs and concerts'. The change wasn't complete, and it certainly wasn't instant, but it reveals itself in a number of observable ways. For instance, up to this point there have been only brief and fragmentary recorded examples of Lester playing a song's melody (on a number of Billie Holiday pieces, for example), but each of these four numbers begins with a full statement or paraphrase of the tune. On the two faster titles, 'Indiana' and 'Tea For Two', he keeps quite close to the original, lightly filling in the spaces and twisting the odd phrase into a new shape. The effect is to change the entire feeling of the two tunes (respectively a barber-shop ditty of 1917 and a light-romantic duet from the musical comedy *No, No, Nanette*) from brightly optimistic to guarded. He does much the same on 'I Can't Get Started', but 'Body And Soul' is a different matter. Here he improvises around the melody almost from the start. This, of course, is what happens on the famous Coleman Hawkins recording, and there are other indications that Lester cannot banish Hawkins from his mind. He even chases chromatic chord changes with arpeggios, for instance in the last bar of the bridge, in a manner thoroughly untypical of him. It is a testimony to the power of Hawkins's creation that it holds sway even over a mind as original as that of Lester Young. The four numbers were recorded on twelve-inch discs, instead of the customary ten-inch, which gave them a playing time of around five minutes each – another innovation.

Despite its lack of recordings, the reputation of Lee and Lester Young's band grew and spread, largely via radio, and in the summer of 1942 it was offered a four-week engagement at Café Society Downtown, in New York. Café Society was a most unusual place. Founded by Barney Josephson, an idealistic former shoe salesman from Trenton, New Jersey, it was set up specifically to defy the informal but widespread segregation at places of entertainment. Its pugnacious motto was 'The Wrong Place for the Right People', although it could equally well have been 'The Right Place for the Left People', because the club attracted its customers from the city's left-wing intelligentsia. Many of the old stereotypes still lingered in the popular mind, but progressive opinion had moved on since the 1920s. Socialism preached the brotherhood of man, which meant equality of the races, and Josephson's brave enterprise was widely applauded. It was successful because there were more left-inclined people in New York City than anywhere else in America. Jazz was not the only entertainment on offer. Along with singers such as Lena Horne and Billie Holiday, there were musical comedy artists and even the occasional concert pianist.

Figure 9. 1942 (1 September). Opening night for Lee and Lester Young's Band at Café Society Downtown, New York City, with (l to r): Lee Young (drums), Clyde Hart (piano), Red Callender (bass), Luis Gonzalez (guitar), Bumps Myers (tenor), Guydner Paul Campbell (trumpet), and Lester. Note: instrument now vertical, but mouthpiece still twisted and head tilted to right. (Peter Vacher collection)

To be invited to appear in New York was a definite step up. Apart from Lester, none of the band had played there before. Even the absurdly long hours – 8 pm to 4 am – could not entirely dampen their satisfaction with the job, and they were doubly pleased when the original four-week contract was extended to six months. Since it was now ensconced in the recording capital of the United States, this should have been the moment for the band to make its record debut, but any chance of doing so was scotched by the action of the AFM. A three-sided dispute involving the union, the broadcasting networks and the record companies had been rumbling on for some time, and, on 1 August 1942, AFM president James C. Petrillo called an indefinite strike of musicians against the entire recording industry. It was to last more than a year and cause grievous damage to the very people whose interests Petrillo (described by one historian as 'a self-important, obstreperous, tyrannical little man'[8]) was supposed to be defending. Almost certainly, the strike deprived Lee and Lester's band of the chance to make records.

On 6 February 1943, Willis Handy Young died in Los Angeles, aged seventy-one. Lee, now *de facto* head of the family, was obliged to hurry home to take care of things and Lester went with him. Most band members, having no connections in New York, drifted home soon afterwards. Sarah Young, Lester's stepmother, lasted only two weeks longer than her husband. Lester returned to New York after the funerals, but Lee elected to remain in LA. It was the end of their joint band, and they rarely played together after that. Lee went on to enjoy a solid career in music. He was the first black musician to be given a full staff contract with Columbia Pictures, and it was he who taught Mickey Rooney to play the drums for the movie *Strike Up The Band*. He later toured the world with Nat King Cole for almost ten years and went on to work as a record producer and recording executive for ABC Records, United Artists, Motown and other leading companies.

Lester, by contrast, was back exactly where he had been a year ago – no band, no gigs, no prospects. After a few weeks spent scuffling around the New York jam sessions, a job came up with Al Sears and his band. He was back to being a sideman again. His life seemed to be running backwards.

7 jammin' the blues

Al Sears was a tenor saxophonist, a few months younger than Lester, who had been leading a series of bands over most of the preceding decade. His current, thirteen-strong outfit had been formed the previous October for a residency at the Renaissance Casino and Ballroom on West 138th Street. This contract came to an end after Lester had been on board for a couple of weeks and Sears signed up for a long tour under the auspices of the United Services Organisation (USO), a partly state-funded voluntary body which provided entertainment for the troops. With the country on a war footing, shortages of fuel and other supplies were making life increasingly difficult for touring bands. A government-backed USO tour was a valuable engagement in such circumstances. It was a good band, by all accounts, and Al Sears proved a remarkably unselfish leader, handing Lester a large share of the limelight. On the rare occasions in later life when he mentioned his tenure with Sears, Lester was non-committal, but he must have been reasonably content because he remained with the band until it broke up at the end of the tour, on 30 September 1943.

Back in New York, he resumed his regular round of jam sessions, only to be called back temporarily into the Basie ranks to cover for an ailing Don Byas. Basie was currently resident at Harlem's Apollo Theatre, where astonished audiences went wild at the announcement of Lester's name. He must have realized by now that he was something of a star, and the very obscurity in which he had been languishing in recent times may have added to his cachet, turning him into a kind of underground celebrity. Whatever the case, no sooner had the word got round that Prez was back with Basie than Byas returned and Prez vanished once more.

The experimental sessions continued at Minton's, Monroe's and other Harlem clubs. At thirty-four, Lester must have felt like the oldest inhabitant, but he had long been accepted by Dizzy Gillespie, Charlie Parker, Thelonious Monk and the rest as an honorary member of the bebop revolution. When, towards the end of October 1943, Gillespie and bassist Oscar Pettiford had the chance to form a band for a residency at the Onyx Club on 52nd Street, they asked Lester to join them and he accepted – thus becoming a member of what was probably the first regularly constituted and paid bebop band in history. The other members were Harold 'Doc' West, who had played drums in Lester's short-lived band, and pianist George Wallington. Thelonious Monk sometimes took over on piano. To Lester's great delight, Billie Holiday was also appearing at the Onyx, alternating with Dizzy's band.

Meanwhile, back in Basie's camp, Don Byas was drinking heavily. He was a man of notoriously uncertain moods and dangerous temper, and alcohol made him quarrelsome. One night, during a backstage argument at the Hotel Lincoln, he drew a pistol and began waving it about threateningly. Basie sacked him on the spot. Knowing that Lester was playing at the Onyx, a mere eight blocks away, Basie asked Jo Jones to catch him at the White Rose, the musicians' 52nd Street watering-hole, at the end of that night's work and offer him his old job back.

> I went round to the White Rose and got Lester... I bought him a beer and told him, 'You're due at work tomorrow night at seven o'clock. You come to the Hotel Lincoln, etc., etc.' And there he was! Nobody said nothing. He just sat down and started playing... They didn't say, 'Hello, Lester, where have you been?' or nothing. He came back in the band just like he'd just left 15 minutes ago!'[1]

This would have been at the very end of November 1943, almost three years after his abrupt departure in December 1940. One can only guess at his motives. He had apparently turned down several offers from Basie in the interim. Possibly the fact the Byas had been fired played a part. In his mind, as we have seen, being fired was something to be ashamed of. Perhaps he took some satisfaction in quietly returning and taking over the job from which Byas had been sacked. On the other hand, he may simply have decided to swallow his pride. At times he must have regretted his decision to leave the band that had been his home and in which he had been so happy. Those few days in October, substituting for Byas, may well have sparked off a powerful fit of nostalgia.

Apart from a few scrappy off-air fragments by the Lee and Lester band, and the four enigmatic pieces with Nat Cole and Red Callender, we have no sound recordings of Prez between April 1941 and this point, and nothing substantial since his last Basie session of August 1940. Largely, of course, this was as a result of the AFM strike, but in any case Lester had been away from New York, where recording activity was concentrated. The strike was now gradually drawing to a close, as record companies negotiated new deals with the union, and he was back in New York. Even so, left to himself, Lester might not have taken advantage of the changed circumstances. But, returned to the bosom of the Basie clan, he was once again at the centre of the jazz world and caught up in its dynamism. In no time at all he was back in the studios.

The first session, on 21 December 1943, was for Signature, a small label catering to dedicated swing lovers, with a seven-piece band consisting mainly of Basie-ites, under the leadership of trombonist Dickie Wells. Always a perfect partner for Lester, Wells performs here with the grave jocularity that marks all his best work. The intervening years had brought no significant change in his style, except perhaps to see his tone grow riper and more vocal and his invention more vivid. One can almost feel Lester's relief at being once more in such company as he unfurls solo lines of effortless grace and formidable ingenuity. In fact, like all the small-band recordings from this period involving Lester Young, the four numbers ('I Got Rhythm', 'I'm Fer It Too', 'Hello Babe' and 'Linger Awhile') recorded at this session are quite exquisite. No longer in the vanguard, but with their styles fully mature, musicians such as Wells and trumpeter Bill Coleman perform with magisterial aplomb. Possessed of more robust personalities than Prez, they had emerged into early middle-age full of confidence. Nevertheless, even in such company, his are the solos which stand out.

On the evidence of these four pieces we can tell that the changes in Lester's playing, discernable on the Cole–Callender records, were no temporary aberration. To begin with, the tone is noticeably thicker and grainier. How this came about we do not know. Various explanations have been advanced, including mechanical ones involving reeds, mouthpieces, instruments, even recording techniques. Reeds regularly wear out and, like all professional saxophonists, Lester devoted care to choosing and looking after them. He used Rico 2½ cane reeds, and there is no evidence that he made any radical departure from these until his last few years, when he took to using plastic reeds, with somewhat mixed results. Throughout his first Basie period, Lester used the same mouthpiece, a metal Otto Link. He was still playing on it during his time with Al Sears, according to the single surviving band photograph from mid-1943, so it must have been the one he used on the Cole–Callender session in July 1942. At some point in the latter part of 1943 he switched to a Brilhardt 'Ebolin', made of black ebonite with a white plastic strip across the upper surface. This is clearly identifiable in photographs dating from 1944 onwards. He could have made the change for reasons of tone, but comfort may have been the deciding factor. Lester had sensitive teeth and it has been suggested that the plastic inlay may have absorbed some of the vibration.

Photographs of Lester taken throughout his first and second Basie periods show him playing a Conn tenor saxophone dating from the early thirties, a model known as the 'Big Bore'. Towards the end of his life he was pictured playing a later Conn model, the 10M, and on one occasion a Selmer 'Super Action', which was probably a gift for promotional purposes. No significant advances in recording technique had been made between 1940 and 1943. So, apart from some possible minor effect brought about by switching mouthpieces, we can rule out a purely mechanical explanation. But, even so, the sound changed.

Reed instruments differ from all others (except for the harmonica, the kazoo and the swannee whistle) in that they are actually taken into the player's body. Strings and percussion are operated at a distance, and even brass instruments lie against the outer edges of the lips. The saxophone, being a reed instrument, goes inside the player's mouth, not far (a couple of centimetres at most), but it is enough to establish a mysterious intimacy. What goes on inside there? Once the jaws close and the lips form an airtight seal, that sliver of cane and wedge of metal or plastic become a temporary part of the human physiognomy. The diaphragm pushes the lungs, air is expelled, the reed vibrates and its movement resounds in the mouth cavity, the teeth and the intricate labyrinth of sinuses. The most precise and delicate movements a human being can make take place inside the mouth, and there, in that secret place, the saxophone player creates his sound. Perhaps that is why, as jazz writers are always telling us, the saxophone, of all instruments, most resembles the human voice.

Our voices convey far more than words. They betray our feelings, our age, our confidence or lack of it, even our state of health. They are *us*, physically and spiritually, and the uncanny parallel between voice and instrument extends to this as well. In this context it is interesting to note that historians of the opera sometimes refer to the 'darkening' of Caruso's voice around the year 1908, the tone changing from a light *bel canto* to a heavier *tenore di forza*. Enrico Caruso was aged thirty-five in 1908; Lester Young was aged thirty-four in 1943–4.

If Lester's sound no longer expressed the buoyant optimism of former years it was probably because he no longer felt buoyant or optimistic. The changed sound is accompanied by simpler and more deliberate phraseology. The youthful suppleness of the late 1930s has been replaced by a certain caution. The jauntiness which had so captivated him in the playing of Frankie Trumbauer has all but evaporated now. In its place something far more complicated is starting to emerge, an ambivalent mixture, suggesting, among other things, regret, longing, uncertainty, wry humour and hope diluted by experience. The gap in his recorded work serves to emphasize a change which had no doubt been a gradual process, but the outcome is clear. Over the course of a few years, Lester Young had unwittingly succeeded in extending and deepening the language of jazz. Before him, the music had dealt in strong but fairly straightforward emotions – feeling good, feeling bad – but in his playing from the mid-1940s onward, we begin for the first time to encounter emotional ambiguity. It was born of his own extreme sensitivity and no other jazz musician's work has ever been so emotionally transparent, or so devoid of rhetorical defences.

Exactly a week after the Dickie Wells session, Lester was recording again, this time for a new label, Keynote. This is the first session to feature Lester alone, accompanied by the standard piano-bass-drums rhythm section, and the four numbers from it are generally regarded as being among his best work. The first, 'Just You, Just Me', offers an instructive contrast with the youthful 'Shoe Shine Boy' because, whereas that was impetuous and optimistic, this is gentle and ruminative. In 'Shoe Shine Boy' one catches only fugitive glimpses of the original theme. 'Just You, Just Me' begins with a caressing, sparsely decorated exposition of the melody, from which grows an improvised chorus so clear in outline that it seems simply to be another way of looking at the tune. There is none of the old rhythmic flamboyance as he moves with infinite gentleness through the harmonies, approaching their most characteristic points from unexpected directions. Another noticeable difference is in the pitch of the whole piece. More than half the notes are in the lower register of the instrument, whereas in former times he tended to use this region only as a springboard or turning-place for phrases which found their climax in the upper register. This, combined with the thicker tone, imparts a somewhat rueful quality to the piece, but the incisive musical mind is in full working order, following a train of thought which seems obvious when expressed, but which no one else could ever have conceived.

Lester's accompanists on this session were pianist Johnny Guarnieri, who delivers a brisk and supportive variant of Basie's style, drummer Sidney ('Big Sid') Catlett and the bassist Slam Stewart, who played magnificent rhythm bass and also bowed solos, to which he hummed or sang along an octave higher. This was his speciality and he made a point of introducing it at every possible opportunity. As a result, each of these tracks, together with a fair proportion of other small-band records from the late swing era, contains a sample of Slam's party piece. The charm, it must be said, soon palls.

The other pieces from this session are an easy-swinging 'I Never Knew', an up-tempo blues entitled 'Afternoon Of A Basie-ite', in which Lester produces some classic examples of how to swing on a single, repeated note, and a meltingly tender 'Sometimes I'm Happy'. There are two takes of each number, and it is interesting to note that Lester's solos are substantially different each time. In the second take of 'Sometimes I'm Happy' (after an interminable chorus from Slam Stewart), he brings the piece to a close with a beautifully manipulated quotation from 'My Sweetie Went Away'.

Partly as a result of wartime conditions, the Basie band's work-pattern had changed. Instead of strings of one-night shows, entailing daily road travel over long distances, they now played at least a week in one place before moving on. This made life a great deal easier. Better still, the band now had several long-term residencies in New York. It was during these periods that the small-band sessions were recorded. Most of March 1944 was passed at the Roxy Theatre, during which time two sessions took place, one for Keynote, on 22 March, and the other for Commodore on the 28th.

The band for the four Keynote numbers ('After Theatre Jump', 'Six Cats And A Prince', 'Lester Leaps Again', 'Destination KC') was billed as the Kansas City Seven, and it was indeed exactly the group which had recorded under that name in September 1939, except for the bass player, Rodney Richardson, who had replaced Walter Page in the Basie orchestra. (For contractual reasons, Basie himself appeared this time under the pseudonym 'Prince Charming'.) A comparison of Lester's playing in the first and second incarnations of the Kansas City Seven reveals just how radically it had changed in less than five years. Compared with the fine-grained sound of 1939, his tone sounds almost brash. This is particularly noticeable in the vibrato, which has become very pronounced. Generally speaking, jazz musicians use 'terminal vibrato', which starts from practically nothing and intensifies towards the end of a note. In Lester's case, the fast, shallow terminal vibrato of his early years grew deeper and more intense. The first four bars of his solo on 'After Theatre Jump' consist of essentially the same one-bar phrase repeated four times, each ending on E-flat (piano D-flat) and held for two beats. Compare the strong terminal vibrato on those four notes with the barely perceptible shiver at the ends of long notes in, say, 'Lester Leaps In' by the first Kansas City Seven and the difference is quite remarkable.

His improvised line is also different, incorporating alarming leaps from one extremity of the instrument's range to another and the use of strange intervals, such as the beboppers' flattened fifth, which turns up more than once in 'After Theatre Jump'. His whole approach has become more dramatic, with notes frequently bent or slurred, and the use of an extraordinary upward glissando, a rising ululation covering an octave or more, that has an air of urgency, almost desperation, about it. Lester's playing on the Commodore session ('Three Little Words', 'Jo-Jo', 'I Got

Rhythm', 'Four O'Clock Drag') displays very much the same characteristics. He is not quite as adventurous on this date, but supremely elegant nonetheless, especially in the blues 'Jo-Jo'. The music from both sessions is classic late swing – poised, confident and relaxed. The only missing element is Lester's clarinet. Somewhere along the way he had lost his old metal instrument and had not found a replacement.

It is impossible to guess at Lester's feelings about being back in Basie's band. On the one hand it represented the failure of his attempt to become a bandleader in his own right, although he was probably reconciled to that by now. On the other, there was the pleasure of being back in the old routine among so many friends. A few familiar faces were missing, including Walter Page, who had temporarily retired from the fray, and Buck Clayton, who had been drafted. Fortunately, Buck was stationed near New York and able to make the occasional recording date, hence his presence in the revived Kansas City Seven. Lester soon resumed his position as the band's joker. He acquired a small bell, which he would ring when anyone made a mistake. If he made a mistake himself, everyone else within reach would make a grab for the bell. Lester's private language now included the term to 'ring the bell' on someone, meaning to catch them out. The expression soon spread to jazz insiders and became current hip usage for a while.

The band's long engagements at the Lincoln Hotel's 'Blue Room' were hailed as something of a breakthrough. Prestigious hotels in midtown Manhattan were reluctant to hire black bands. Even if the management itself was not prejudiced, it would usually be afraid of upsetting prejudiced customers. But, according to Basie, in his memoirs, the owner of the Lincoln, Miss Maria Cramer, was an independent-minded woman. She admired Basie and the band and refused to be daunted by convention.

> Whenever she would get a little flak about having us in that kind of room, she would say, 'I'm sorry, but I want the Count in there. I'm very pleased with the Count.'
>
> I will always remember how she used to come backstage every night during one of our intermissions. I would look up and there she was.
>
> 'Well, are you going to take a little walk and have a little nip?'
>
> 'I'm with you, boss lady!'
>
> 'No, I'm with you, pal!'[2]

Basie's record label, Columbia, was one of the last to settle with the AFM, so the band had not yet resumed commercial recording. Fortunately, the Blue Room was provided with a radio link and during the band's second stint, which lasted throughout April and May 1944, it broadcast regularly over both the Mutual and AFRS networks. Surviving off-air recordings reveal that Lester was heavily featured as a soloist. Sometimes he sounds almost like his younger self, while at others he is clearly the Prez of 'After Theatre Jump'. There are so many of these Blue Room recordings (around 170 items at the last count, of which about half have been made commercially available) that choosing individual examples is difficult. To take a few almost at random: a very fast version of 'I Found A New Baby', dating from 10 April, includes a gloriously airy and agile Lester solo in the classic style, while that on 'Blue Room Jump' (date uncertain), is filled with honks, false-fingering, smears and upward glissandi. There is even an occasional solo at ballad tempo, something which never came Lester's way during his first Basie tenure. His gentle half-chorus on Thelma Carpenter's vocal feature, 'Call Me Darling', is quite delectable.

The sound quality of the Blue Room broadcasts is generally fairly good, although variable. There are, however, a few studio recordings by Basie's band dating from Lester's second tenure where the quality is less hit-or-miss. One set, made for the Savoy label on 18 April, is billed as by Earl Warren and his Orchestra, which is actually the Basie band without Basie, under the leadership of its lead alto saxophonist and occasional vocalist. Prez solos sweetly on three of the four numbers. There are also sessions for the government-owned V-Disc label, provided for the exclusive use of US forces, and for Lang-Worth, a company which recorded music on sixteen-inch discs for sale to radio stations. Lester Young solos are scattered liberally throughout these, together with those by Buddy Tate, providing the same kind of stylistic contrast which had marked the earlier partnership between Prez and Herschel Evans.

Two further small-band sessions were recorded during the second Blue Room residency. The first, also for Savoy and on the same date as the Earl Warren session, appeared under the billing 'Johnny Guarnieri's Swing Men'. It also featured trumpeter Billy Butterfield and clarinettist Hank D'Amico, with Guarnieri leading the rhythm section of Dexter Hall, Billy Taylor and Cozy Cole, on guitar, bass and drums. It is particularly well recorded and captures the texture of Lester's tone and the subtleties of his articulation to perfection in all four numbers ('These Foolish Things', 'Exercise In Swing', 'Salute To Fats' and 'Basie English'). The way he opens 'These Foolish Things', moving delicately from literal statement of the melody to pure improvisation in the course of sixteen bars is particularly graceful. This was his slowest recorded tempo so far, the harbinger of much that was to follow.

In fact, only two weeks later he recorded the first of his acknowledged ballad masterpieces. Once again it was a Savoy session, this time with Prez as the only soloist, accompanied by Basie and the regular rhythm section. The piece in question is 'Ghost Of A Chance', an uninterrupted solo, without even a piano introduction, lasting forty-eight bars, at a tempo of fifty-six beats per minute. This is so unlike anything he had done with Basie before that it cannot have been a casual choice. Its beauty lies in its completeness as a musical utterance. It conveys not just a vague mood, but a precise state of mind; not mere gloom or sadness but something more akin to weary resignation. The song's full title, '(I Don't Stand) A Ghost Of A Chance (With You)', probably helps explain how Lester came to choose it. There is also the fact that the whole harmonic flavour of the piece is dominated by the chord of the augmented fifth, which occurs five times in the course of its thirty-two-bar chorus, the chord whose plaintive uncertainty he had always found attractive. Lester dwells on the chord, unambiguously spreading it out, sometimes with a hovering ninth for good measure. The whole centre of gravity is low, rising only occasionally into the instrument's upper range with reluctant effort, which further intensifies the mood. On a few occasions the improvised line touches briefly on notes which, coming from anyone else, would sound like the chromatic substitutions of the young beboppers. Here, though, as the line droops a semitone below where you might expect it, the effect is of a soft, melancholy sigh. Two takes of 'Ghost Of A Chance' exist, of which the first is the classic version. The other three titles ('Blue Lester', 'Indiana' and 'Jump Lester Jump') are considerably more energetic. Lester's fluency, sharpened by the instinctive rapport between himself and Basie, is as beguiling as ever.

The Blue Room engagement ended on 31 May; the band moved on to a string of dates in New England and the extra-curricular small-band sessions ceased. One cannot help wondering what people around the country made of Prez. His distinctive presence is nicely described by Whitney Balliett:

> He had protruding, heavy-lidded eyes, a square, slightly oriental face, a tiny moustache and a snaggle-toothed smile. His walk was light and pigeon-toed and his voice was soft. He was something of a dandy. He wore suits, knit ties and collar pins. He wore ankle-length coats and porkpie hats – on the back of his head when he was young, and pulled down low and evenly when he was older.[3]

The broad-brimmed porkpie hat had become his trademark. Also, according to the singer Sylvia Syms, 'He used cologne and he always smelled divine'.[4] In Harlem or along 52nd Street such a figure would attract attention only from admiring swing fans, but what they made of him in Providence, Rhode Island, or Worcester, Massachusetts is anyone's guess. He was not a garrulous man, which is just as well, because no one outside his own circle understood his personal argot. When he played, he held the saxophone at a forty-five degree angle – 'like a canoeist about to plunge his paddle into the water' is how Balliett described it.[5]

The leisurely tour moved on, first to Chicago (where Lester had to have two weeks off for an operation on his tonsils), back eastwards to Ohio, south-west to Kansas City (a duller and more well-behaved city than in the old days), and finally out to the west coast. They opened at the Orpheum Theater, Los Angeles on 1 August 1944, and who should be there to greet them but the ever-enthusiastic Norman Granz. He had been drafted into the army and then, through a bizarre technicality, discharged. Granz had not been idle. Finding himself back in the film industry, he had got together with the photographer Gjon Mili, hatched an idea for a jazz film, and sold it to Warner Bros. Since neither he nor Mili had ever made a film, this says a lot for his powers of persuasion. It was to be a short, fifteen-minute feature depicting a jam session, and Granz had been waiting eagerly for Basie's band to arrive in LA so that he could sign Lester up to appear in it.

And so it was that, some time during the first two weeks of August 1944, Lester, Jo Jones, Harry Edison and Dickie Wells, along with a number of resident LA musicians, turned up at the Warner Bros studios in Burbank to record the music for *Jammin' The Blues*, as the movie was to be called. The Basie band then moved north, to spend three weeks in San Francisco and Oakland, and Mili and Granz used the time in choosing which numbers to include and setting up the film sessions. They had recorded far more music than they needed, and used far more musicians than were strictly necessary – but why not? This was Hollywood, after all, and it would make a nice change for black jazz musicians to benefit from some of the movie capital's largesse. Even so, the film would be absurdly cheap to make, which was just as well, since Warner Bros seem to have had misgivings about it from the start. Besides Lester, those seen in the film are Illinois Jacquet (tenor saxophone), Harry Edison (trumpet), Marlowe Morris (piano), Barney Kessel (guitar), Red Callender and John Simmons (bass), Big Sid Catlett and Jo Jones (drums). Marie Bryant appears in a singing and dancing role, partnered in the latter by Archie Savage. The shooting took place during the second or third week of September, after Basie had returned to LA, to play the Plantation Club in Watts.

Behind the opening credits the screen is dark, save for some drifting smoke and a pattern of two lighter, concentric circles. On the soundtrack a piano plays the blues. An off-screen voice announces: 'This is a jam session. Quite often these great artists gather and play ad lib hot music. It could be called a midnight symphony.' The camera pulls away and down, revealing the circles to be the brim and crown of a wide-brimmed pork-pie hat. Under the hat is Lester Young. He raises the saxophone to his mouth and begins to play. From this very first image, it soon becomes clear that, from a visual point of view, *Jammin' The Blues* is wildly avant garde for 1944. Mili was a celebrated still photographer, whose work appeared regularly in *Life* magazine, and this was a new departure for him. He disregards the conventional assumption that a filmed scene is the straightforward portrayal of an actual event. Lester, for instance, is first seen playing alone in an empty space, but when the camera returns to him he is sitting in the middle of the band. This is where he is found at the start of the final number. The camera then cuts to Marie Bryant and Archie Savage dancing – and there's Lester, standing alone behind them, saxophone at a forty-five degree angle, blowing a solo, a plume of smoke rising from the cigarette clamped ingeniously between two fingers of his left hand. (Smoke seems to have been a vital ingredient of arty photographs in those days. Elsewhere there's a long, loving shot of Lester getting a cigarette out of the packet, striking a match, lighting up, shaking the match out and exhaling a prodigious cloud.) Each image is beautifully composed and meticulously lit, so that the overall effect is of a series of stills that have miraculously come to life. This visual discontinuity imparts a curiously dreamlike atmosphere to the whole film. Add to that a string of photographic tricks with reflections, multiple images and so on, and you begin to see why Warner Bros felt uneasy about the whole project.

Indeed, the studio made several attempts to interfere. According to one report, Warner originally wanted 'hundreds of jitterbug dancers in a gigantic spectacle of rhythm',[6] whereas Mili and Granz wanted no dancing at all. The brief Bryant–Savage sequence was the compromise they reached. Then there is the portrayal of the musicians themselves, which was intimately tied up with the matter of race. Warner objected to the appearance of Barney Kessel, a white musician, in an otherwise black cast. Couldn't they find a black guitarist? Granz refused to budge. This time they came to the absurd compromise that Kessel should appear either in deepest shadow or as a pair of disembodied hands.

There is nothing revolutionary about the music in *Jammin' The Blues*. It is pure late swing – poised, fluent and self-assured. Lester himself plays beautifully in all three numbers, the opening slow blues, the closing fast blues and Marie Bryant's vocal feature, 'On The Sunny Side Of The Street', to which he contributes a heart-breakingly tender half-chorus.

Figures 10 and 11. 1944. Smiling amidst the drifting smoke – an out-take from *Jammin' The Blues* – plus a few frames from the movie, featuring Lester in action. (Frank Driggs collection)

Jammin' The Blues was released towards the end of the year and received a nomination in the Best Short Film category of the 1944 Academy Awards. It is important not only because it captures Lester Young at a high point in his creative life, but because it was the first film to present jazz as an art which defined itself in something like its own terms. And it arrived at exactly the right moment. A new jazz audience was growing, with a new sensibility. It did not want to dance to the music, or even be entertained by it, in the conventional sense. It wanted to be a part of it – to be there in the smoky, midnight back room, where the real stuff was played. This was the audience of would-be initiates to which *Jammin' The Blues* was addressed, an audience which would grow to huge international proportions in the post-war years. Perhaps instinctively, Norman Granz had detected these early stirrings of a phenomenon on which he would soon build an empire.

8 DB blues

Jammin' The Blues catches Lester Young at a creative peak, and also on the brink of his personal abyss. Just before the shoot he had received his call-up papers. This was not the first communication the Draft Board had sent him, but he had taken no notice. A touring musician was a moving target and, as Buddy Tate explained: 'A lot of musicians beat the Draft by saying, "Well, I didn't get it – I was on the road." We were all trying to stay out because we were making too much money, and there were so many lonely ladies.'[1] This time, however, the Draft Board really meant business.

> So, the FBI found out where we were going to be. We were playing three months in Watts, and this young guy came out one night – zoot suit on, big chain down to the knees like Cab Calloway. He introduced himself, and we thought he was a fan. He stayed all night, and he said, 'I'd like for you and Lester and Sweets and Jo to be my guests'. And he bought drinks and drinks and drinks all night. And at the end he pulls this badge and shows it to Lester and Jo Jones. 'Be at this address at nine o'clock in the morning or we'll come and get you and you'll go to jail for five years.'
>
> I said not to worry, because by this time Lester's drinking a quart of 100 per cent proof a day, and they won't want Jo either, because he's crazy. But, man, the next day they put them in.[2]

The date was Monday 25 September. Lee drove Lester to the Draft Board office on 8th Street, where his appearance and demeanour seem to have aroused the suspicion that he was putting on an act in order to be rejected. With his hat, long coat and dark glasses, his tiptoe gait and incomprehensible speech, not to mention his impressive record of draft avoidance, it was at least a possibility. There was little enthusiasm for military service among the African-American population, and to get out of it, by whatever means, was widely regarded as a victory over the system. There were several popular songs on this very subject, the most witty being Nat Cole's 'Gone With The Draft', in which he celebrates his own good luck in having flat feet, while mocking the fate of his less fortunate compatriots. Flat feet, bad backs, obscure nervous conditions, dubious sexual orientation, strings of dependent relatives – all these and more were paraded daily before increasingly sceptical Draft Board officials. The upshot was that both Lester and Jo were passed on into the induction process. Among Lester's many unusual personal traits was his habit of always telling the truth. As a child, he had been proud of being a 'good kid'. His mother had taught him that lying, stealing and cruelty were wrong, and he accepted this as a rule of life. So when he was asked routine questions about drugs and alcohol he answered, quite candidly, that he smoked cannabis and drank whisky daily and in large quantities. Almost certainly, this marked his card with the authorities. Then came the medical examination, which revealed not only that he was spectacularly unfit, but that he suffered from epilepsy and had apparently contracted syphilis at some time in the past. At this point it was decided that he should have a 'spinal', a lumbar puncture. The prospect terrified him and he became so agitated that he was put into a padded cell overnight.

A few days later, now labelled 39729502 Pvt. Young, Willis L., he was sent to Fort Arthur, California, to begin his basic training. By now he had become utterly desperate and did what he had always done when faced with intolerable situations: he ran away. On the night of Saturday 30 September, Lee Young (who, as it happens, had escaped military service by pleading a bad back) was about to begin playing the opening set at the Downbeat Club when, glancing round, he caught sight of his brother, lurking in the wings. Grabbing Lester, he dragged him into his car, drove to Fort Arthur and bundled him over the wall, back into the camp.[3]

It is hard to believe that any army in the world would want Lester Young as a recruit. Quite apart from the undeniable facts of his alcoholism, his epilepsy, and his generally deplorable physical condition, at thirty-five he had reached the age limit for being drafted. Several people attempted to point all this out to the authorities. Lee tried, Norman Granz tried, Basie's manager, Milt Ebbins, tried, but all to no avail. After a few weeks at Fort Arthur, Lester was moved to Fort Ord, where an army photographer took a posed publicity picture of him and Jo Jones, apparently jamming together, and finally to Fort McClellan, Alabama. Here, he was required to negotiate an assault course, during which he fell and injured himself severely enough to be detained in the camp hospital, for what reports describe as 'minor rectal surgery'. His conduct thus far had been so un-soldier-like that the camp shrink, or Chief of Neuro-Psychology, Dr Luis Perelman, took the opportunity of inspecting him. He concluded that Lester was in a 'constitutional psychopathic state manifested by drug addiction (marijuana, barbiturates), chronic alcoholism and nomadism'.

The good doctor could not suggest what might be done about this parcel of afflictions, so he acted like the seasoned soldier he was and passed the buck. He concluded that here was a 'purely disciplinary problem and that disposition should be effected through administrative channels'. So far, Lester had not been accused of anything, apart from falling on his backside, so it is hard to know quite what the 'problem' was supposed to be which might be disposed of by disciplinary means.

Alerted no doubt by Perelman's helpful comments, the battalion commander, Captain William Stevenson, decided to keep an eye on Lester when he was discharged from hospital. After a few days he noticed Lester looking somewhat the worse for wear and asked him how he was feeling. Lester, dedicated truth-teller that he was, replied that he was 'high'. Stevenson asked what had brought about this condition and Lester showed him a handful of pills. The captain sent for Lester's company commander and together they searched Lester's locker. There they discovered pills, cannabis and a pink liquid that smelled of alcohol, all of which were sent away for analysis. It has been rumoured that they also came across a photograph of Mary Dale, which Stevenson (a Southerner) found highly objectionable. All kinds of apocryphal details have attached themselves to the tale of Lester's army experiences, most of them, like this one, quite feasible but unsubstantiated. What is certain is that Lester was arrested and charged 'according to the 96th Article of War' with possessing habit-forming drugs without a valid prescription. Preparations for his court martial were put in hand.

Now a second psychiatrist, Lawrence J. Radice, peered into Lester's psyche and was distressed by what he found therein. 'During his early life his school and family adjustment were poor', he reported. Lester had hardly ever been to school and had been summarily snatched from his mother at the age of ten, so Radice was spot-on there. 'He has been arrested several times' the report continued, 'and at present has a common-law wife'. This may be the origin of the rumour about Mary Dale's picture, although what business it was of the army's is anyone's guess. There are further remarks about drink and drugs, concluding with: 'In view of his undesirable traits and inadequate personality, he is unlikely to become a satisfactory soldier.' Buddy Tate could have told them that at the very beginning, but now that the opinion was official the solution was obvious – let him out. But when Lester's court martial convened on 16 February 1945, the army was too bemused by the spectacle of what it had recruited to be in any fit state to see the obvious.

The details of this whole episode came to light in 1980, in consequence of the US Freedom of Information Act. A summary and partial transcript of the court martial was published in *Down Beat* magazine's January 1981 issue. It reveals a degree of mutual incomprehension woeful to behold.

In the circumstances, Lester's appointed defence attorney, Major Grimke, did quite a good job. After eliciting from Captain Stevenson the circumstances surrounding the arrest, he called for an account of Lester's interrogation from the investigating officer, Lieutenant Humphreys. This revealed the fact that Lester had voluntarily told the Draft Board and its medical officers all about his drink and drugs habits. Characteristically, he had been at pains to point out that he 'had never harmed anyone'. When it was Lester's turn to speak in his own defence, Grimke led him through the events surrounding his injury. From this it emerged that he had been allowed no period of recuperation, but had been sent from hospital straight back to training, carrying a full pack, rifle and cartridge belt. He was currently also suffering severe withdrawal symptoms. In short, Grimke succeeded in establishing that the army had recruited Lester in the full knowledge of his unsuitability as a soldier, and that by returning him to duty directly from hospital it had been in breach of its own laid-down procedures. The prosecution seemed interested only in finding out where Lester had obtained his illegal supplies.

The entire proceeding took just over an hour and a half, at the end of which the bench of four military judges returned a verdict of guilty by a majority of three to one. Lester was sentenced to be dishonourably discharged, to forfeit all pay, and to serve a year in the military detention barracks at Fort Leavenworth, Kansas. The routine review of the case, submitted at the end of the month, found the sentence appropriate, because the use of unauthorized drugs was an offence. It did, however, note that: 'Testimony of the accused indicates that he used drugs during the past ten years, *that the Draft Board knew it at the time of his induction*, and further he cannot get along without them' (my italics). In other words, the army had made a mistake but refused to back down or make amends. We should not be surprised at this. Military justice was not the same as civilian justice. The commanding officer appointed legal officers to act as counsel for the prosecution and the defence, also the judge and jury or, as in this case, the bench. The judicial process was a product of the chain of command, and thus weighted in favour of the authorities. In such circumstances, the defence could not really develop its own case, but was limited to reacting to the case presented by the prosecution. If Major Grimke could have cross-examined members of the LA Draft Board, the medical officer who sent Lester out to the training ground straight from hospital, the psychiatrists and others, the case might have been dismissed or he might have been discharged from the service without punishment. But that would have brought the judicial process into conflict with military discipline, and so could not be allowed to happen. That is what sealed the fate of Private 39729502 Young.

Throughout World War II, the US armed forces constituted a strictly segregated institution. The common view among unsophisticated whites, that Negroes, however amiable and well-meaning, were irresponsible, childlike and not to be entrusted with important tasks, lay at the heart of the military's attitude in racial matters. Thus it was that, among the 200,000 black US soldiers in 1942, the overwhelming majority were to be found doing non-technical jobs in Quartermaster and Engineer Corps units – pumping gasoline, loading trucks, digging ditches and so on.[4] And then there was the question of sending black troops abroad, which was a very hot potato indeed. The authorities felt it incumbent upon them to remind Negroes of their place, and to ensure that they did not learn to act differently when away from home, especially overseas – hence the rigid, even draconian discipline which was meted out to them. The commingling of races, particularly, was a prospect so dreadful to many that it presented the military authorities with a serious public relations problem. Eventually, they feared, pictures of black troops consorting with foreign white women would appear in the papers and support for the war effort, especially in the south, would be undermined. (So, if Mary Dale's picture had indeed come to light during the search of Lester's belongings, it would gravely have prejudiced the case against him.)

In the event, Lester was sent not to Fort Leavenworth but to Camp Gordon, Georgia, which was very bad news. To be confined to a military prison was bad enough, but to be black and a prisoner in Georgia was even worse. Once again, all kinds of tales and rumours have attached themselves to Lester's time in prison. He himself rarely spoke about it, beyond describing it as 'one mad nightmare'. One can only imagine what torture it was for him, a soft, slow-moving man, condemned to a world where everyone shouted and all movement had to be at the double. It is said that he was beaten up on several occasions, either by drunken white guards or black fellow-prisoners. On one occasion, according to Jo Jones, Lester tried to run away, or rather he hid behind a bush while out on a working party and thought about running away. But the guards had guns and this was Georgia, and what would he do if he succeeded? He couldn't hide for the rest of his life, not in his profession. So he came out from behind the bush before anyone noticed he was missing. There was a band at Fort Gordon, which he was not officially allowed to join, although it seems that friends smuggled him in from time to time, without the authorities finding out. The arranger and composer Gil Evans happened to be stationed at a nearby military hospital, where he worked in the dispensary. He managed, by devious means, to slip Lester occasional gifts of whisky and cannabis. Evans, of course, was white and such actions were particularly hazardous when they took place across the colour-line.

The war in Europe ended with the surrender of German forces on 7 May 1945, and in Asia with the dropping of atomic bombs on Hiroshima and Nagasaki on 6 and 9 August. Both victories had been achieved without the aid of Pvt 39729502 Young, still languishing in the detention barracks at Fort Gordon. He was released with something over two months of his sentence yet to be served, although exactly when he was let out remains a mystery. Official records state that he received his dishonourable discharge on 15 December, but a news item in *Down Beat* of 15 November announces his recently having signed a recording contract with the Philo label. The most likely explanation is that he was allowed to leave but remained officially a member of the armed forces for a number of weeks afterwards. This was common practice and ensured that departing conscripts remained under military discipline until they are well clear of base, and thus restrained from unseemly behaviour on leaving. Whatever the case, his clothes and possessions were returned to him and Norman Granz paid his fare back to Los Angeles. His only comment on arrival was, 'I'm out. That's all that matters'.

9 jumpin' at mesner's

The three-year contract with Philo, a new label, had been negotiated by Norman Granz on Lester's behalf while he was still confined at Fort Gordon. Towards the end of the war, small record labels seemed to be springing up almost daily. The dispute between the AFM and the record companies had led to a curious state of affairs, in which anyone who was ready to agree to the AFM's terms could obtain the union's approval and set up in the record business, while established major companies which held out remained strike-bound. This produced a vast bubble of tiny enterprises run by dreamers, sharp operators, would-be tycoons and ambitious fans, few of them with any real expertise. Some didn't even have offices and reputedly kept their paperwork in their hats.[1] Compared with this Dickensian rabble, Philo's proprietors, the brothers Eddie and Leo Mesner, were paragons of good business practice. Lester Young was their first contracted artist.

The exact date of Lester's first post-army recording session is uncertain, but it definitely took place during the first half of December 1945. From the way he plays, you would hardly guess that he had just been through the worst year of his life. His technique is sharp, his imagination fully engaged, his tone, if anything, tighter and more controlled than in some of his immediately pre-army recordings. This is recognizably the Lester Young of 'Ghost Of A Chance' and *Jammin' The Blues*. Apart from Lester himself, the band consists of trombonist Vic Dickenson, pianist Dodo Marmarosa, bassist Red Callender and drummer Henry Tucker. Four pieces were recorded – 'DB Blues', 'Lester Blows Again', 'These Foolish Things' and 'Jumpin' At Mesner's'. They all contain excellent performances, but 'These Foolish Things' is exceptional. Lester seems to have had a particular fondness for this song and played it often. In this version he barely touches on the original melody but begins his improvisation immediately after the piano introduction, as Hawkins does in his classic version of 'Body And Soul'. Nevertheless, to anyone familiar with the original, this is still recognizably 'These Foolish Things'. It follows the harmonies which give Jack Strachey's melody its distinctive flavour, creating a kind of shadow version which, in its shape and colouring, is archetypal Lester Young. Lester's approach to material such as this makes a fascinating study in itself. To draw an analogy with painting: if the original tune is the subject and the jazz musician's playing of the tune is the painter's treatment of that subject, then Lester's treatments vary enormously. It has already been noted that his 'Just You, Just Me', of December 1943, begins close to a literal portrayal of the melody and follows it closely throughout. His first recording of 'These Foolish Things', from April 1944, begins with a clear likeness and gradually moves away from it as the improvisation proceeds, while the December 1945 recording is almost entirely 'abstract'. It is also more buoyant than, say, the magnificent but sombre 'Ghost Of A Chance', covering the instrument's full range in bold, energetic strokes.

It used to be claimed, by critics who cannot have been listening very carefully, that Lester's army experiences had proved so traumatic and damaging to his psyche that his playing thereafter was a shadow of its former self. His time in Fort Gordon certainly affected him badly and caused him to become suspicious and withdrawn, but his playing in the immediate post-war period was anything but lacklustre. 'These Foolish Things' is a beautiful piece of work, as is 'DB Blues' (ironically named after the Fort Gordon detention barracks). This is based on a forty-four-bar pattern consisting of two twelve-bar blues choruses, the bridge of 'I Got Rhythm' and one further blues chorus. He creates an effect of lazy nonchalance with his lagging phrases, but there is nothing lazy about the playing on 'DB Blues'. It is secure and purposeful and packed with the surprising twists and turns that mark all his best work. Indeed, 'DB Blues' turned out to be a minor hit, and not just with jazz buffs either. Its relaxed, late-night atmosphere struck a chord in post-war black California. It summed up, in its quiet way, a spirit of ease and freedom, of getting mellow in some little dive, of not having to wear uniform or jump out of bed at the crack of dawn. For former soldiers, and those still looking forward to the day when they could achieve that most coveted promotion of all, to the rank of ex-serviceman, it was a siren song. There is another version of 'DB Blues', recorded for the AFRS show *Jubilee*, aimed at black service personnel, in which the announcement of the title brings forth a chorus of rueful chuckles from the studio audience. They may not have known about Lester's experiences in the DB, but they recognized a dedicated ex-serviceman when they met one.

During these early weeks of his regained freedom, Lester appears to have been making up for lost time. For Philo (soon to be renamed Aladdin) he recorded the session mentioned above, followed by one with a band accompanying Helen Humes and then another under his own name. The Helen Humes date is pleasant enough, although Lester plays few solos. His second session as leader finds him accompanied by a seven-piece band playing neat, well-rehearsed backing figures behind him on three of the four numbers, 'It's Only A Paper Moon', 'Lover Come Back to Me' and 'Jammin' With Lester'. There's nothing here which rises quite to the level of 'These Foolish Things' or 'DB Blues', but he sounds relaxed and happy, and someone has obviously taken trouble over the arrangements.

Norman Granz had entered Lester's professional life in 1942. He had produced Lester's first solo recording session and featured him in the film *Jammin' The Blues*. Now he was helping him get his new career started by overseeing his first few recording sessions for Philo/Aladdin. Granz was driven by two passions – to bring jazz before the public and to challenge racial prejudice – and he was a man who got things done. From putting on public jam sessions in small clubs he had taken the big step, in July 1944, of hiring the 2,800-seat Los Angeles Philharmonic Auditorium for a jazz concert in aid of a defence fund for a group of young Mexican-American men falsely accused of murder. The evening was a sell-out and Granz was encouraged to mount regular jazz events at the same venue, under the series title 'Jazz At The Philharmonic', or 'JATP' for short. On 28 January 1946 he put on his most ambitious show yet, a 'Down Beat Award Winners' Concert'. Only two actual winners could be rounded up, saxophonists Willie Smith and Charlie Ventura, but Charlie Parker and Dizzy Gillespie happened to be appearing in Los Angeles at the time and Granz managed to get them, too, along with Lester and other notables. It was the first time that Lester Young and Charlie Parker appeared together on the same stage.

These early JATP shows were presented as public jam sessions and deliberately unstructured. Almost every number amounted to a desultory theme statement followed by a long string of solos, and with such a large audience there was a tendency for musicians to play to the gallery. Granz had the proceedings recorded and the results, in the cold light of day, prove to be more than somewhat mixed. Of all the front-line soloists, Lester is by far the most poised and coherent. Even on 'Sweet Georgia Brown', taken at a lunatic tempo of around 300 beats per minute, he sounds calm and collected. His phrases balance elegantly and he does not coarsen his tone – unlike Parker, who seems to be having a particularly bad time with a squeaky reed. The show was a sell-out and everyone enjoyed it, except the management of the Philharmonic Auditorium. They banned any further JATP shows in the hall, ostensibly on the grounds that some of the audience had got up and danced in the aisles, but Granz suspected that the spectacle of racially mixed performers playing to a racially mixed audience had finally proved too much for them. Nevertheless, he knew that he was onto something big and was determined to continue presenting such concerts. And no one could stop him using the JATP title, which was on its way to becoming an established brand-name.

In late March or early April 1946, Granz arranged a studio session for a trio consisting of Lester and Nat Cole with Buddy Rich playing drums. Lester and Nat had been playing together quite often since Lester's release, on AFRS *Jubilee* shows and elsewhere, and obviously enjoyed one another's company. It was a mistake on Granz's part not to include a bass player on the session, because when Cole is playing the accompanying role he is reduced to simple vamping in order to keep the rhythm going, and when he takes a piano solo a disconcerting hole appears in the rhythmic texture. Nevertheless, it sounds a joyous occasion, especially the faster numbers, where the lack of a bass is less obvious and sheer momentum helps to keep the thing airborne. Lester's series of solo breaks at the start of 'I Found A New Baby' recalls the *joie de vivre* of his early Basie career. For some reason, the eight numbers recorded at this session[2] did not appear on Philo/Aladdin. It is possible that it was done without Mesner's knowledge. It may be that Granz was already planning to launch his own record label and intended these pieces as part of his stockpile.

Granz organized the first JATP tour to start in Los Angeles on 22 April. It travelled around California, from San Diego to San Francisco, before heading for Chicago's Civic Opera House, on to New York for three Monday nights at Carnegie Hall and back to Chicago for a final show on 22 June. The cast included both Lester Young and Coleman Hawkins, with Buck Clayton on trumpet, Kenny Kersey (piano), Irving Ashby (guitar), Billy Hadnot (bass) and Buddy Rich (drums). This band recorded a *Jubilee* session on the afternoon of the opening night and everyone played very well indeed on all three numbers – 'I Got Rhythm', 'Lady Be Good' and 'Sweet Georgia Brown'. One feature of these informal presentations was the constant repetition of the same core repertoire. It is a tribute to the ingenuity and imaginative energy of these musicians that they always seemed able to find something new to make out of a dozen or so standard tunes and the twelve-bar blues.

The tour proved to be a great success. Granz had sensed the beginnings of a change in the public perception of jazz, back in the war years. His jam-session nights in clubs had shown that a generation had arrived which identified closely with the music. The first JATP shows had proved that there was a considerable audience in southern California, and the tour had proved that the same applied in other parts of the US. He was soon to discover that the phenomenon was equally strong elsewhere – in Canada, Western Europe, Japan, Australasia and even the nations of the Soviet bloc. Jazz was about to enter upon its Golden Age, with Norman Granz as its biggest impresario. From the very beginning, his artists travelled first class, stayed at the best hotels and never played to segregated audiences. He also paid very well indeed.

Back in Los Angeles, Lester recorded another session for Aladdin in August, with a quintet consisting of pianist Joe Albany, one of the early pioneers of bebop, guitarist Irving Ashby, bassist Red Callender and drummer Chico Hamilton. All four numbers[3] are excellent, but 'You're Driving Me Crazy' is exceptional. Once again, Lester dispenses with the original tune to create a long, continuously evolving melody of formidable ingenuity. By contrast, the ballad 'She's Funny That Way' appears in a very close, sensitively expanded paraphrase.

Lester had been based in Los Angeles since leaving the army. His benefactor, Norman Granz, was there and so was his record label, Aladdin, but New York was where he really wanted to be. He was also ready to have another try at leading a band. Soon after the above session, he made the move to New York City. This time he was less casual in his methods and, before beginning to build his new band, sought out an agent. Moe Gale, who signed him up, had an impressive track record. His clients included such popular artists as Cab Calloway, Ella Fitzgerald and the Ink Spots, and he had the exclusive booking contract for the Savoy Ballroom. When it came to assembling the band, Lester followed his previous course of spotting talent at jam sessions. In this way he found the young pianist Argonne Thornton and drummer Lyndell Marshall. Rodney Richardson, who had been in Basie's band during Lester's second stint, and had played bass on the 'Ghost Of A Chance' session, left Eddie Mallory's band at the Savoy to join Prez. On guitar was Fred Lacey, who had been a fellow prisoner in the Fort Gordon detention barracks, and whom Lester valued as a friend as much as anything else. The final recruit was trumpeter Maurice 'Shorty' McConnell, formerly of the Earl Hines and Billy Eckstine orchestras. They rehearsed in September and Moe Gale had them booked into Chicago's Hurricane Lounge, starting on 3 October.

The band proved so popular that its one-month engagement was extended to two, and it was in Chicago that it made its record debut. Not even his most ardent fan would have called Lester's band a slick outfit. On the evidence of the six pieces recorded for Aladdin in October 1946, there was very little in the way of arrangement and what

ensemble passages there were consisted mainly of unison theme statements. Lester is very much the focus of attention, although the others
all have plenty of solo space. Three of the numbers are twelve-bar blues
('SM Blues', 'Jumpin' With Symphony Sid' and 'No Eyes Blues'), two are
standards ('Sunday' and 'On The Sunny Side Of The Street') and one is
a riff based on the 'I Got Rhythm' sequence ('Sax-O-Be-Bop'). Although
he seems to have taken little interest in formal arrangements, it would
be a mistake to assume, as many have, that Lester merely walked onto
the stand, called the numbers and played his solos, leaving the band
to get along as best they could. If that were the case, why do two of
the blues numbers contain prepared changes of key? 'SM Blues' opens
with two choruses in F from the rhythm section, drops to D-flat for
Lester's first two choruses and moves up a tone to E-flat for two more,
remaining there until the end. 'Jumpin' With Symphony Sid' (named
after the New York jazz disc-jockey, 'Symphony' Sid Torin), opens with
two choruses from Lester, followed by two from Argonne Thornton, all
in the key of C, switching suddenly to F for two more from Lester and
the closing theme. Apart from the F to D-flat, which is a venerable Basie
trick, it is hard to see the rationale behind these changes, which would
not be at all obvious to the casual lay ear, but they certainly didn't occur
by accident. (Dick Hyman, who played with Lester some years later,
recalled that he would call out instructions, such as 'three Cs and two
Fs' before embarking on a number.[4]) 'Sax-O-Be-Bop' is the same tune
as Billy Strayhorn's 'Frolic Sam', which had been in the repertoire of the
Lee-and-Lester band. The unison theme is pretty scrappy, but the solos
are fine. The styles of both McConnell and Thornton were firmly in the
bebop camp and, while neither is a particularly exciting improviser,
their ability is never in question.

The outstanding performance from this first session by Lester Young
and his Band is the ballad, 'On The Sunny Side Of The Street', which
Lester plays solo throughout. From the number of times he chose to play
it, he obviously loved this old revue song by Jimmy McHugh and Dorothy
Fields. In its original form it is an optimistic, cheer-up ditty, but to him it
seems to have signified the opposite. He plays the first few notes, a rising
phrase intended to signal brightness and hope, with a kind of yearning
melancholy which he develops over a chorus and a half with a wealth of
delicate inflection. How anyone, faced with such artistry, could possibly
have concluded that Lester Young in 1946 was a burnt-out case is beyond
understanding.

10 'von hangman is here'

During his five weeks in Chicago, at the Hurricane Lounge, Lester met the woman who was to become his next wife. Her name was Mary Berkeley and she was African-American. Little is known about her life before they met, but by all accounts she was a quiet, calm person, the precise opposite of the volatile Mary Dale. They were married towards the end of 1946. Mary was just the kind of companion Lester needed at that stage in his life. His army days were behind him, but a legacy of bitterness and suspicion remained. He found it hard to trust people, especially white people whom he didn't know well, and tended to avoid socializing if at all possible. He had, of course, always been shy. His mother, Lizetta, believed that it was his shyness that had started him drinking in the first place.[1] Now, after the horrors of Fort Gordon and the detention barracks, the shyness seems to have grown into something resembling full-scale agoraphobia. Jesse Drakes, Shorty McConnell's successor on trumpet in Lester's band, recalled that he refused to eat in restaurants, insisting that food be brought to him backstage or in his hotel room. 'He thought people were looking at him,' Drakes said.[2] One of the most telling phrases in Lester's private language was 'I feel a draft', meaning that he detected racial hostility. He had always been sensitive to such drafts and now this sensitivity expanded to obsessive proportions. To express it, he coined a new phrase of almost Jacobean resonance: 'Von Hangman is here'.

Lester had learned one hard lesson from his first, brief experience of leading a band, namely that he was hopeless when it came to the practical side of the job. Moe Gale quickly arrived at the same conclusion, and proposed that Lester should have a personal manager to look after his day-to-day business. The man selected for the job was Charlie Carpenter, formerly a singer with Earl Hines's band and co-writer, with Hines, of 'You Can Depend On Me', which Lester had recorded with Basie, back in 1939. He knew the music business from the inside, possessed a methodical mind and had an authoritative manner. Lester felt he could rely on him. With Moe Gale taking care of the bookings and Charlie Carpenter permanently on hand, Lester Young's band was a successful going concern. Throughout 1947 and 1948, it toured the country, from New York to San Francisco, Seattle to Fort Worth, playing a mixture of one-nighters and brief residencies, drawing sizeable audiences and making quite good money. In the autumn of 1947 Mary gave birth to a son, also named Lester and universally dubbed 'Little Lester'. The family moved into a comfortable new apartment on 140th Street, in the modestly prosperous sector of Harlem popularly known as 'Strivers' Row'. The apartment block boasted such status symbols as a uniformed doorman and a carpeted lobby. In these years Lester Young, with his famous hat, became something of a celebrity. The August 1949 edition of *Ebony* magazine carried a photo-feature entitled 'How to Make a Pork-Pie Hat', which showed Lester going through the various stages of pinching and folding a broad-brimmed hat to produce the trade-mark shape. Yet, despite all these marks of success and Lester's undoubted popularity with the paying customers, a faint but discernable whine of dissatisfaction arose from the music press and some jazz insiders. Much of it boiled down to simple disappointment that Lester's new band wasn't a reincarnation of the Kansas City Six. John Hammond, for instance, complained that, whereas Lester had once been surrounded by his peers, he now worked with juveniles and nonentities. *Down Beat* and *Metronome* reviewers kept up a thin drizzle of complaint, claiming that Lester's playing was lacklustre and the band under-rehearsed. A notable exception was Ralph Gleason, *Down Beat*'s west-coast correspondent, who was bowled over by the band's performance in San Francisco in February 1948, mentioning 'the wonderful, wonderful Lester Young solos', and concluding his review with: '...given a chance, this band might click in a rather big way'.[3]

Recorded evidence tends to bear out Gleason's view. For example, on 8 November 1947, Lester's band shared a concert stage at New York Town Hall with the twenty-four-year-old rising star, Sarah Vaughan. *Down Beat*'s Mike 'Mix' Levin, reviewing the show, complained that Lester played out of tune, was bereft of ideas, 'wallowed around the stand' and that it had been a 'pathetic' performance all round. He seemed to attribute this to Prez not being in 'perfect physical condition', presumably his euphemism for 'drunk'.[4] Well, he certainly doesn't play out of tune on the live recording, nor does he sound short of ideas. His playing on 'Lester Leaps In' is a particular delight, especially the interplay with his sparky new drummer, twenty-three-year-old Roy Haynes, while 'These Foolish Things' is quite thrilling in its fusion of passion and inventiveness. As for the rest of it, Prez certainly sounds remarkably jovial – singing along with Thornton's piano introductions and cracking jokes with the band – but by no means drunk, or even 'over-refreshed'. To be fair to *Down Beat*, the magazine must have shown Lester the review in advance and asked him to comment, because it prints a reply from him in the same issue. In it, he goes over the top in the opposite direction, claiming that this had been 'the greatest concert I ever played in my life'.

Whatever the case, the critical complaints reached such a pitch that Aladdin decided to record Lester's last session under their contract using a specially hired rhythm section of sharp young players – pianist Gene DiNovi, guitarist Chuck Wayne, bassist Curly Russell and drummer Tiny Kahn. No decision could have been calculated to upset Lester more. In the first place, it was as good as telling him that his regular band, personally chosen by him, wasn't up to the job. Secondly, three of the four newcomers were white men whom he scarcely knew. According to the critic Leonard Feather, who had been commissioned to select the band and produce the session, 'it was a less than comfortable afternoon'.[5] It began with Lester muttering a tune title and immediately starting to play. Somebody, possibly DiNovi, suggested mildly that it might help if everyone knew what they were supposed to be doing, whereupon Lester stared blankly at a point on the wall about two feet above DiNovi's head and said wearily, 'If Prez's kiddies were here, the kiddies would know what to do'. (He had taken to referring to himself in the third person.) Matters proceeded in a similar vein, but they managed to get four numbers down.[6] One of them, 'East Of The Sun', is rather a good performance, although Prez deliberately trails off at the end instead of finishing cleanly.

The sheer illogicality of it all must have been very perplexing to Lester and those around him. Not so long ago, before the army hiatus, he had been a failed bandleader, struggling along as a sideman in other people's bands or sharing leadership with his brother, and often hard-up, a hero to young musicians and jazz insiders but otherwise getting nowhere. That had all changed now. He was a successful bandleader, not rich but comfortably off, married, with a baby son, and living in a nice apartment. Moreover, he had managed to accommodate himself to the new bebop idiom and worked quite happily with musicians twenty years his junior, unlike many of his contemporaries, who had become bewildered and bitter about the changes that were taking place. And yet all that critics and opinion formers could do was complain that he wasn't playing the way he used to, back in the 'good old days'.

Lester found this a constant source of annoyance, and when he was interviewed by the jazz press the subject tended to come up sooner or later:

I have a lot of trouble on the bandstand. They come up and ask me, 'How come you don't play like you played when you played with Basie?' Well, that's not progressive, you know. If I'm going to stay here and play that same stuff year after year, well, Jesus, I'll be an *old* man, you know? So I don't think like that... I have to think of new little tricks and little new sounds and things like that. That's the way I live.[7]

He summed up his attitude in one of his most quoted remarks: 'I try not to be a repeater pencil, you dig?',[8] and it was all part of his concern with originality. Like many highly accomplished and original artists, Lester could never quite understand why other people couldn't do what he could do. In interviews, a mixture of irritation and bafflement seems to enter his tone of voice when questions of originality or artistic influence crop up:

The trouble with most musicians today is that they're copycats. Of course you have to start out playing like someone else. You have a model or a teacher and you learn all he can show you. But then you start playing for yourself, show them that you're an individual, and I can count those who are doing that today on the fingers of one hand.[9]

You got to have a style that's all your own. A man can only be a stylist if he makes up his mind not to copy anybody... Originality's the thing. You can have tone and technique and a lot of other things, but without originality you ain't really nowhere. Gotta be original![10]

His advice to young musicians was, 'You can't be in the choir till you've learned to sing your own song'.[11]

Sometime in the autumn of 1948 there were several changes in the band's personnel, when Shorty McConnell, Argonne Thornton and Fred Lacey left. Jesse Drakes and Freddy Jefferson came in on trumpet and piano respectively, and guitar was dropped from the line-up in favour of Ted Kelly on trombone, making a third voice in the front line. The date-book remained encouragingly full, touring interspersed with quite long stints at major jazz clubs, especially the Royal Roost in New York, from which its sets were regularly broadcast. Surviving off-air recordings are full of invention, with many fascinating hints that Lester had absorbed some of the phraseology of bebop. Typically, however, when these turns of phrase crop up they are rarely quite what they seem. There is a particularly nice one in a version of 'Ghost Of A Chance', from the Royal Roost broadcast of 27 November 1948, in which he plays a phrase which might be a bebop commonplace – it sounds like a common lick based on a flattened fifth substitution – but on close examination it turns out to be built on a far less dissonant note, the flattened ninth of the dominant seventh. With typical Lester Young sleight of hand he tricks the unwary ear into hearing what isn't there. One is reminded of Rudolph Nureyev's oft-quoted dictum, that a great dancer is not the one who makes a difficult step look easy, but the one who makes an easy step look interesting.

Figure 12. 1949. Lester Young and his Band at Birdland, with (l to r), Ted Kelly (trombone), Lester, Tex Briscoe (bass), Jesse Drakes (trumpet), Roy Haynes (drums). Not visible, Freddy Jefferson (piano). Note: instrument vertical and head no longer tilted. (Frank Driggs collection)

The new band (with Junior Mance replacing Jefferson at the piano) made its official recording debut at a session for the Savoy label on 23 June 1949. The results provide an exemplary contrast with those of the fraught afternoon the previous year. This time Lester had his 'kiddies' around him, and glowering resentment was replaced by busy concentration. In fact, so keen does he seem to have been to get exactly the right routine to create the best three-minute performance, that most of the session was taken up with just one twelve-bar blues number. All the successive takes of this were retained and subsequently issued, so we can follow its evolution in detail. The process entails changes to the order of solos, the introduction of riffs and backing figures, followed by their alteration, redeployment or abandonment, solo breaks, key-changes, introductions and codas, all tried and reworked. The whole lot eventually came out under three titles – 'Crazy Over JZ', 'Blues 'n' Bells' and 'June Bug'. One other piece was recorded, a very fast, themeless improvisation on 'All Of Me', entitled 'Ding Dong'. Lester plays tirelessly and elegantly throughout, never significantly repeating himself, and performs quite sensationally in all three takes of 'Ding Dong', energized by the dynamic drumming of Roy Haynes.

This Savoy session was an isolated event, made possible by the fact that Lester was currently without a recording contract. In September, however, he signed with Norman Granz, who had just set up his own label, Clef Records (initially released under the Mercury banner). He also signed up for an extended tour with JATP, thus establishing the pattern of his professional life for the next few years. This consisted of JATP tours of up to two months, interspersed with periods leading his own band and others when he worked as a guest artist, or visiting soloist, at jazz clubs. This arrangement had a destabilizing effect on the band, leading to frequent changes of personnel, but otherwise worked well.

Touring with JATP in its fully-fledged state proved to be a novel experience in itself. The artists travelled first-class, sometimes in specially chartered planes, and stayed at the best hotels, as befitted their status as stars. Whenever questions of racial discrimination or segregation arose, Granz stoutly refused to budge from his declared position: such practices were not to be countenanced, no matter what difficulties might ensue. He would, if the need arose, hire a plane and fly the entire troupe out immediately after a show. In the light of this admirable stand, Lester's conduct must have seemed strange, even disloyal. He would rarely stay in the luxurious accommodation offered, but, whenever possible, take himself off to a small, black-run hotel. The reason he always gave was that he 'didn't want any trouble'. The prospect of rows and arguments, especially in this problematic sphere, terrified him, as it always had.

A JATP tour was renowned as being the most lucrative engagement in jazz. Musicians earned in a night roughly what they could earn in a week at a jazz club, with very little outlay in the way of expenses. A six- or seven-week tour would bring Lester around $5,000, compared with between $800–$900 (less expenses) at clubs over a similar period. A tour was also a high-profile affair, attracting a lot of valuable publicity, both national and local. When JATP was due in town, local record stores would stock up with records by the artists concerned, so record royalties might eventually be added to the proceeds of the tour. All this was very welcome, but there were drawbacks. The atmosphere at a JATP show was often more akin to that at a rock concert of more recent times than at a jazz club. Big audiences in big venues called for broad gestures, simple outlines and overt excitement. Tempos tended towards the frantic, trumpeters went in for high-note pyrotechnics and tenor saxophonists either honked or squealed. None of this was natural Lester Young territory, although, to oblige Granz, he did indulge in a certain amount of half-hearted honking. It was in the 'ballad medley', when each soloist played a chorus of a slow ballad, that he came briefly into his own.

The sudden improvement in their financial position enabled the Young family to give up their Manhattan apartment and buy a house, 116-12, 168th Street, St Albans, in the borough of Queens. Life with the Youngs assumed all the outward appearance of suburban normality. In the opening paragraph of a *Down Beat* interview, Nat Hentoff presents a picture of Lester as head of the household which is so normal as to seem positively bizarre:

> On a recent Saturday afternoon at his home in St Albans, Long Island, Lester Young was alternately watching television and answering questions. Eight year-old Lester Young Jnr had gone to the movies. The pet of the house, a seven year-old Spitz named Concert ('We got him on the day of a concert') was in quizzical attendance. Making coffee was Mary, Lester's wife; also present was the astute, outspoken Charlie Carpenter, Lester's long-time friend who has been with him since 1946 and has been his manager since 1948...[12]

To Prez, this way of life was new and totally unfamiliar. He was now in his forties and had passed virtually his entire existence in that state characterized by the army shrink as 'chronic nomadism'. Just as a British colonial administrator might have continued the habit of a lifetime by dressing for dinner in some tropical outpost, so Lester brought to his new-found role of paterfamilias all the casual profanity of the wandering hipster. Among his St Albans neighbours were two elderly ladies, pillars of the local black church. Sunning themselves one afternoon on their porch they beheld the heart-warming sight of Lester and Little Lester throwing a ball to one another in the back yard. Eventually they tired of their game and turned to go indoors. Lester tried the handle. The door wouldn't open. The fond father chided his son gently: 'There you dumb motherfucker, see what you did? You done shut the door and locked us both out the house!'[13]

Once he was signed to Granz's label, Lester began recording quite regularly, either with his own band or with members of the current JATP cast. His records from this final decade of his life have frequently been written off by critics, or damned with faint praise, which is quite wrong, although their quality is admittedly patchy. His health, both physical and mental, became increasingly precarious during the 1950s, and this was reflected in his playing. The matter was described very well by pianist Dick Hyman, who played with Lester's band at Birdland early in the decade: 'It was a kind of weary-but-still-trying way of playing, it seems to me. Weary, but still somehow with bursts of energy... Not the straight-ahead way he played on the early Basie records, but looser and, I guess, not so tight and inventive as his early days'.[14]

Always highly responsive to his accompaniment, Lester plays quite magnificently on three sessions from 1951–2,[15] where John Lewis is on piano. Lewis was the pianist in Lester's band for something less than a year, during which it functioned mainly as a quartet, without Jesse Drakes. The bassist was Joe Schulman and the drummer Joe Clark, later briefly replaced by Gene Ramey and Jo Jones. John Lewis possessed extraordinary sensitivity and at times seems to be reading Lester's thoughts. He anticipates and knits together Lester's phrases in a way that is little short of telepathic. This often sets off a kind of musical hide-and-seek, as the wily Lester attempts to evade the piano's prompt-ings, pursuing a course which doesn't so much follow the harmonies as brush against them in passing. His playing on all seventeen of these recorded pieces, especially the masterly 'Undercover Girl Blues', is so beautiful and accomplished that one scarcely knows where to begin. The tone is clear, delicate and infinitely flexible. The slurs, shadings and tonal shifts emerge not as applied effects but as organic components of an immensely subtle improvised line. Lewis later spoke of playing with Lester as 'a tremendous adventure all the time. There was always surprise.'[16]

He enjoyed listening to records by singers, of which he had a large collection, and kept up with the latest songs on the radio. He was especially fond of Frank Sinatra ('Frankie-boy', as he called him), Dick Haymes, Jo Stafford and, of course, Billie Holiday. This in turn influenced his choice of material, and it is possible to make a reason-able guess at what had caught his ear from the tunes he chose to play. In amongst the blues and established jazz standards he would drop the occasional unexpected pop item, such as 'Lavender Blue' (a hit for Dinah Shore in 1948) or 'Destination Moon' (Nat King Cole, 1951). Taking just the first three Clef sessions, between September 1949 and March 1951: of the ten songs included, six come from vocal records or films released in the previous two years.[17] In addition, 'September

In The Rain' had recently been an instrumental hit for the George Shearing Quintet, while 'Polka Dots And Moonbeams', which Lester plays with fragile delicacy, had been an early success for Sinatra with Tommy Dorsey's Orchestra.

He chose these songs because he liked them *as songs*, not simply as raw material for improvisation. This was not the fashionable attitude in jazz circles at a time when the distinction between 'serious' jazz and mainstream popular music was being strenuously promoted by the new generation of musicians and critics. His insistence on the importance of knowing the words of a song was even more at odds with progressive opinion:

> A musician should know the lyrics of the song he plays, too. That completes it. Then you can go for yourself and know what you're doing. A lot of musicians who play nowadays don't know the lyrics of the songs. That way, they're just playing the changes. That's why I like records by singers when I'm listening at home. I pick up the words right from there.[18]

Lester made his first foreign tour in the spring of 1952, with a JATP package. There was a sticky moment during preparations for the trip, when inoculations were being administered. He panicked at the sight of the needle and much soothing persuasion was needed before he would submit himself to the ordeal. The tour visited Scandinavia, Holland, Belgium, France, Switzerland and Germany and was rapturously received. It was universally agreed that Lester's best moments came in his slow ballad features, usually either 'These Foolish Things' or 'I Cover The Waterfront'. During a three-day rest in Paris he sat in every night at Left Bank jazz clubs where, by common consent, he played tirelessly and with all his old fire. 'We discovered that Lester could still blow when he wanted to, when he was in the proper environment or mood', commented the French critic Charles Delaunay.[19] After one such night he confided to a French admirer: 'There are too many people at the concerts and I don't think my music interests them. They've come for something else. I bore them. I prefer to play for people who like my music.'[20] In fact, Lester often said that he preferred playing for dancers, where there was a clear if unspoken relationship between them and the musicians. He certainly arrived at a fairly jaundiced view of concert audiences. 'The people look up and they don't know if you're playing good or bad', he said once. 'Sometimes you'll put on an act and they'll clap when you're playing bad.'[21]

Figure 13. 1952. An inscrutable Prez steals the scene in this photo-call for the Jazz At The Philharmonic cast at Amsterdam Airport, with (l to r) Hank Jones (piano), Roy Eldridge (trumpet), Flip Phillips (tenor), Chuck Wayne (guitar), Norman Granz, Max Roach (drums), Lester, Oscar Peterson (piano), Irving Ashby (guitar). (Frank Driggs collection)

Despite this, the JATP team was a happy one. However undiscriminating the audiences may have been, however the critics may have carped, Lester enjoyed the unreserved respect and affection of fellow musicians such as Oscar Peterson, Barney Kessel, Ray Brown (whom, for some reason, he dubbed 'Lawyer Brown') and J.C. Heard. In such company he could relax and be his old, eccentric, joking self. It was in these circumstances that, on 28 November 1952, he recorded his one and only vocal performance. This lay forgotten in the vaults, until disinterred decades later, and allows us a tiny, fleeting glimpse of the relaxed tomfoolery which must have enlivened backstage life with JATP, the kind of thing that musicians quite often get up to while waiting for something to happen. The recording begins with Lester already embarked on singing 'It Takes Two To Tango' (a current hit for both Pearl Bailey and Louis Armstrong), with the rhythm section providing a deliberately corny accompaniment. After a while he seems about to stop and someone calls out, 'Go on! Go on!', which he does, following the vocal with a saxophone chorus, after which the piece shuffles to a halt, amidst laughter. The following dialogue then takes place:

Lester (incredulously): 'You want me to open up *singing*?'

Granz (over the studio intercom): 'Just like you did before. And a little funky intro, Osc.'

Lester (indignantly): 'There's ladies out here!'

Granz: 'Huh?'

Lester: 'You said "funky intro". There's ladies out here.'

Granz: 'Uh-huh'.[22]

In its original sense, the word 'funky' referred to unpleasant body odours of an intimate nature,[23] and was not a term to be used in mixed or polite company. At the time of the above exchange it was beginning to acquire the secondary usage in jazz parlance of 'simple and unsophisticated, in the old, down-home blues style'. Granz was using the second meaning, while Lester was assuming the first. Lexicographers may one day find this accidentally preserved and precisely dated fragment useful.

Granz obviously wanted to record Lester's vocal performance and release it as a novelty item. Lester, equally clearly, had no intention of allowing anything of the kind. His way of squashing the idea was typically sidelong. He sang his vocal chorus, but affected to forget the words, substituting 'drop your drawers!' and a few other mildly vulgar phrases. In 1952 that was enough to make the number unusable. It was released for the first time in the late 1980s.

JATP tours were occupying more and more of his time. There was a further long, three-month trek around the US in the latter part of 1952. A regular stop on these tours was Minneapolis, and it was probably on such occasions that Lester visited his daughter, Beverly, who would now have been in her early twenties. In general, though, he must have found the whole thing tedious, playing the same numbers in the same routine, with just a chorus-and-a-half of his featured ballad each night. It seems that he was now drinking even more heavily and growing increasingly depressed. He felt undervalued and ignored. 'I just don't feel like nobody likes old Prez', he complained to pianist Horace Silver. His physical health was suffering, too. His condition must have worried Mary because, when a further five-week European tour was announced, beginning on 15 February 1953, she decided to travel with him. According to press notices, his playing on the tour varied from inspired at the outset to desultory by the end.

Granz had managed to book two shows in London, despite a long-running dispute between the British and US unions which effectively prevented American musicians from playing in Britain. The concerts were arranged as charity events, for the relief of victims of a recent disastrous flood. Backstage at London's Gaumont State Theatre, Lester told one reporter: 'I'm tired of all this noise... I've nothing against this country, but all this rushing around! I'm losing my weight. Man, I'm so tired!'[24] He did, however, succeed in endearing himself to fellow saxophonist Ronnie Scott, whose band opened the show. Holding out a large German beer stein, he offered it to Scott, raising the lid to reveal a bundle of neatly rolled joints. 'Eyes?' he enquired, politely. Scott took one. They both lit up, inhaled deeply and slowly exhaled. 'Bells?' murmured Lester, with a solicitous smile.[25]

'Weary but still trying'. Dick Hyman's observation catches the state of affairs exactly as Lester approached his forty-fifth birthday. The records constitute a diary of his ups and downs, dispatches from the front. Sometimes the news is encouraging, sometimes not, but on the whole morale seems to be slipping.

11 prez returns

Back in 1934, when Lester had been under pressure in the Fletcher Henderson band, with Mrs Henderson breathing down his neck in her efforts to turn him into an imitation Coleman Hawkins, Billie Holiday had tried to cheer him up by assuring him that, one day, people would be copying *him*. Her prediction had now come true. Al Cohn, it will be recalled, had been captivated by Lester's playing in 1938, at the age of thirteen. He was not alone. In the days when Lester was riding high with the Basie band his tenor saxophone was heard by millions on records, in person and via the radio. Many of these listeners were very young, and some of them were themselves destined to take up the tenor saxophone. Lester never suspected it (because who, in the days before teenagers were invented, paid any attention to what kids thought?), but a quite extraordinary number of them were profoundly affected by his music. They thought it was the most beautiful thing they had ever heard and made up their minds to follow him. During the years when Lester was playing with Lee on the west coast, through his second Basie period and while he was incarcerated in the detention barracks, they were growing up, the best of them getting their first jobs in bands. With so many men away in the forces, jobs were quite easy to come by. When Lester emerged from the Army at the end of 1945, there they were, rank upon rank of them – young, bright, devoted.

By a strange quirk of history, on 14 December, the day before Lester's official discharge, one of these disciples, eighteen-year-old Stan Getz, with a six-piece band under the name of Kai's Krazy Kats, recorded four pieces for Savoy. They amounted to a respectful pastiche of the previous year's Kansas City Seven records, with Getz in the Lester Young role. Some time later, Lester heard Getz sitting in with Ben Webster at a 52nd Street club and complimented him. 'He said, "Nice eyes, Prez. Carry on",' Getz recalled. 'He called me "Prez"!' Prez had recently taken to calling everyone he approved of 'Prez', but Getz took it as a benediction and treasured it for the rest of his life.[1]

Lester's spiritual children – Stan Getz, Al Cohn, Zoot Sims, Dexter Gordon, Wardell Gray, Paul Quinichette, Allen Eager and many more

– came from many races and backgrounds, and eventually from many nations. One of them, Brew Moore, a white boy from Mississippi, where black and white still scarcely acknowledged each other's existence, spoke for them when he declared, 'Anyone who doesn't play like Lester is wrong!' Some even imitated his mannerisms. They cultivated his cool gaze and detached manner, and even the curious, forty-five degree angle at which he held the instrument. As he grew older, the angle grew less acute, but, for a while, the mouthpiece remained twisted, so that he was playing with his head tilted to one side. All this emulation should have made him happy but it didn't. A less complicated man would have smiled proprietorially at the devotion shown by his followers, and even crowed a little over this final proof that he had been right all along. But the whole business just made Lester nervous. His view of 'copycats' has already been aired, but he found the attention of these sleek young men to be especially dispiriting because what they were echoing was his younger, happier self. He must have found their sheer energy painful to behold, although he couldn't help but admire some of them. To Leonard Feather, in 1950, he admitted grudgingly: 'If you're talking about the grey [white] boys, Allen Eager, he can play.'[2] And in one ragged live recording by Eager from April 1947, a jam session broadcast over station WNEW in New York, we can hear what Lester heard which caused him so much anguish. In his solo on 'Sweet Georgia Brown',[3] Eager is the youthful Lester to the very life – poised, relaxed, confident and resourceful. His tone is almost exactly that of 'Taxi War Dance', the articulation so clean and precise that it makes you want to shout with delight. It is the music of a young man telling his story. To Lester, such performances were a cruel, ever-present reminder of his own youth. 'They're picking the bones while the body's still warm', he remarked glumly.

His flagging spirits received a boost in July 1953, when his name appeared among the winners in the annual readers' poll of *Metronome* magazine, albeit in third rather than first place. He did, however, get to take part in that year's recording by the 'Metronome All-Stars'. He can be heard playing a somewhat distant obbligato to Billy Eckstine in a vocal rendition of 'St Louis Blues', and two sprightly choruses in an up-tempo instrumental version of the same number.

Nevertheless, this was not a happy time for him. His playing had always intimately reflected his life, 'told his story'. Now it seemed that part of him, his voice, was being taken from him. How could he use it to tell his story when others were using it to tell theirs? Booked to play opposite Paul Quinichette, whose sedulous imitation had led to his being dubbed the 'Vice-Prez', Lester turned in desperation to Charlie Carpenter.

'I don't know whether to play like me or Lady Q, because he's playing so much like me.'[4] And on being informed that someone else 'sounds just like you', he asked bleakly, 'Then who am I?'[5] Instead of flattering him, the imitation left him baffled and confused. He drank even more and his playing became more and more introspective. But as the years passed, it became clear that many of the disciples were following exactly the course which Lester himself had approvingly outlined. They had begun by imitating him but gradually developed their own distinct voices. In fact, his was not the only influence acting on their generation; there was also the huge, unignorable fact of Charlie Parker, whose complex harmonic vocabulary exerted an equally strong pull. Throughout the late 1940s and well into the 1950s, jazz tenor saxophone style flourished in glorious diversity under the twin attractions of Lester's cool detachment and the bustling chromaticism of Parker's bebop. These were the years in which jazz first began to attract a dedicated worldwide audience and, as it spread, that cool sound, mediated particularly through the recordings of Stan Getz, entered deep into the fabric not only of jazz but of popular music in general.

Meanwhile, Lester's own recordings betray an uncertain state of affairs. In December 1953 and almost exactly a year later he recorded sessions with his own band. From the first comes a masterly version of 'Tenderly', in which he lays out the melody in a characteristically knowing and allusive way and picks up after the intervening trumpet and piano solos exactly where he left off, bringing the piece to a beautifully modu-lated close. But whenever the tempo rises above a medium bounce he runs into difficulty. Something seems to be interfering with both his technique and his thought processes. He struggles manfully through 'Lady Be Good', but fails to get airborne, and his intonation is woeful at times, as witness the final few bars of 'Willow Weep For Me'. The following December's session starts with a sunny piece called 'Another Mambo' (actually a variation on 'St Louis Blues'), cast in the novel form of alternating passages in a minor key against a Latin-American rhythm and swinging twelve-bar blues. It is happy, optimistic and immaculately performed, yet the very next number to be recorded is a doleful and defeated-sounding 'Come Rain Or Come Shine'. It is not helped by the fact that Lester had now taken to using plastic reeds. These have a ten-dency to retain tiny drops of condensation between their surface and the mouthpiece, causing the sizzling sound sometimes called 'frying up'. Lester's later recordings are full of examples, and sometimes he uses the slight buzz to expressive effect, but here it just hangs around like radio interference.

There was another long JATP tour in the fall of 1955, during which Lester made friends with the youngest musician in the company, eighteen-year-old Bobby Scott, pianist with the Gene Krupa Quartet. He bestowed the name 'Socks' upon the young man (Bobby Scott/bobby-socks/Socks) and made him his confidant. Twenty-eight years later Scott wrote a wonderfully intimate little memoir of Prez on that tour:

> Even the respect shown him was often perfunctory, and too many musicians seemed merely to suffer him. I suffered, too, reminded by the musicians in an exquisitely subtle way that at my age I was not entitled to an opinion. I've often thought that I came by Lester's friendship as a result. We were both suffered.

> His clothes draped his frame. I took it that he'd lost weight and simply couldn't waste time and money playing at being a fashion plate. There was something rumpled, but not dishevelled, about his appearance. His walk, which was more of a shuffle than an honest walk, had something Asiatic about it, a reticence to barge in. He sidled. It was in keeping with the side-door quality of his nature...

> He was a night person...He *entered* the evening. Even the quantity of his words increased as the light of day waned. It was as if he'd climbed a ridge of small hillocks, then settled into a golden period, a span of bewitched time... His stick-like body, so worn by his utter disregard for its health, straightened to its limit only during those hours of music. And the music turned on his capacity of camaraderie and humour.[6]

The tour ended at the Shrine Auditorium, Los Angeles on 31 October. A recording session held on the following day, featuring six stars of the touring show, yielded disturbing results. Lester sounds frail and confused. His theme statements verge on the incoherent, his solo on 'Red Boy Blues' makes no sense at all, and the lively tempo of 'One O'Clock Jump' is clearly too much for him. He seems to be falling apart before our ears, and his condition is thrown into cruel relief by the smooth perfection of the other participants, especially Oscar Peterson and Sweets Edison. In these circumstances, one is entitled to wonder why Norman Granz allowed him to continue, unless it was to spare his feelings. Shortly after arriving home, Lester collapsed with a nervous breakdown and Mary had him admitted to the psychiatric unit at Bellevue Hospital. He remained there through the remainder of the month and into December.

The treatment, rest, regular meals and temporary withdrawal of alcohol did him good and he emerged in far better spirits. One thing, however, would not be restored. He was never again to have a band of his own. Charlie Carpenter might occasionally book an *ad hoc* group to accompany him for a few nights, but it was to be package shows and solo gigs from now on. With the band out of the picture, the chance now arose to record Lester in some other context. One obvious idea was a reunion session with Teddy Wilson, Jo Jones, Freddie Green *et al.* The notion would certainly be welcomed by Lester's older fans, many of whom had been agitating for something of the sort for years and, even granted his misgivings about being a 'repeater pencil', Lester himself must have found the prospect inviting. The session was set for 12 January 1956 at Fine Sound studios in New York, and the rest of the band consisted of Vic Dickenson on trombone, Gene Ramey (bass) and Roy Eldridge (trumpet). The resulting album, entitled *Jazz Giants '56*, recalls the easy, unbuttoned creativity of those brief months in the mid-1940s, the mellow late-afternoon of swing, before the US Army stepped in and spoiled everything.

The Lester Young of *Jazz Giants '56* is not the Lester of 'Shoe Shine Boy', nor of the Kansas City Seven, nor yet of the early-1950s recordings with John Lewis, but neither is it the incoherent Lester of a few months previously. His phrases tend to be shorter than in earlier days, presumably because his lung-power has declined. His tone is looser, too, with a curious, slightly acrid edge to it, probably a result of the plastic reed. But the hesitancy, gloom and sheer despondent aimlessness of the recent past is banished entirely. He takes the lead on four of the five tracks, playing the opening theme and the first solo, and, gentle though he is, radiates authority. On three of the medium-tempo pieces ('I Guess I'll Have To Change My Plan', 'I Didn't Know What Time It Was' and 'This Year's Kisses') his uniquely tender way with the melody of a song – a slight deviation here, a small decoration there – makes the whole thing simply glow. And the original song continues to shine subtly through the improvisation which follows. This, of course, is a branch of the jazz art which had been brought to perfection by some of the very people present at this session. Playing alongside Vic Dickenson, whose entire style was based around variations on the melody, and Teddy Wilson, that master of firm, understated elegance, was a very different proposition from playing with his 'kiddies', brought up in bebop with its emphasis on hard-edged lines and harmonic elaboration. 'Bebop can be pretty', Lester once remarked, 'but my music is swing'. The one really fast piece on the album, 'Gigantic Blues' (a twelve-bar blues in F major), would have defeated him back in October, but here he sails through his four choruses, riding the beat rather as a seagull rides a stiff sea breeze, using the minimum of movement to maximum effect.

On the following day, 13 January, Lester returned to Fine Sound, in equally good form, to record seven further pieces with Wilson, Ramey and Jones. The results, apart from the blues, 'Prez Returns', were released as an album under the title *Prez & Teddy*. The six numbers are all American classics from the 1920s and '30s,[7] taken at moderate tempos, and each performance could serve as a model of the genre. To choose just one example, 'Taking A Chance On Love' opens with two light but purposeful choruses from Teddy Wilson which are startlingly good, even by his standards. (The piano could have been more in-tune, but you can't have everything.) This is followed by three choruses by Lester which amount to an affectionate excursion through Vernon Duke's simple but imposing melody, with its clear, robust harmonies. One can just imagine the lyric running through his mind as he plays. As is often the case with Lester at his best and most characteristic, there is no division between exposition and improvisation. 'Prez Returns' (included in a later album, *The Lester Young Story*) is a blues in G major, the same key as the earlier 'Undercover Girl Blues', and it is interesting to compare the two. Whereas 'Undercover Girl' is full of delightful evasions and sneaky surprises, 'Prez Returns' is simple and candid. The difference probably lies in Lester's response to the very different accompanying styles of John Lewis and Teddy Wilson.

Now that his own band was no more, much of Lester's work came in the form of 'guest star', or visiting soloist, appearances at jazz clubs around the US. This method of working bears a certain resemblance to Russian roulette, since the soloist very often has no idea what kind of accompaniment will be awaiting him. Bobby Scott tells of walking into a club where Lester was appearing as guest star: 'Oh, Socks, baby, I'm glad to see you here! This boy playing piano plays very well, but he puts in eight changes where there oughta be two.'[8] This was a common complaint, perhaps born from a mistaken eagerness to impress the great man. Lester's requirements of his accompanists were actually quite modest and boiled down to keeping it simple and staying out of his way. The drummer Willie Jones received the following instructions at the start of an engagement: 'Now, behind me all you do is tinkety-boom, tinkety-boom. When the trumpet player comes on you can do whatever you wanna – Boom! Bang! But behind me, tinkety-boom, tinkety-boom, and we got it made.'[9]

The evening of Monday 3 December 1956 found Lester opening for six nights at Olivia Davis's Patio Lounge, Washington DC. The resident Bill Potts Trio were to accompany him, three young men just out of the army, at the start of their professional careers. It was a familiar routine – a brief talk-through with the trio to decide tunes and keys, a request for tinkety-boom etc., and then settle down to the night's work. The thing about this gig was that Bill Potts recorded the final three sessions using professional equipment.

Lester arrived at the club, took one look at the bandstand and saw three microphones, two professional tape recorders, a mixer and a set of headphones. His mouth dropped, he looked at me with a very sad look on his face and said, 'Oh, no, Billy, no! Norman will kill me!'[10]

Fortunately Potts and the trio overcame his misgivings, with the aid of a gift-wrapped bottle of brandy, and two nights' and one afternoon's music was captured on tape. A few fragments escaped onto commercial records over the years, but it was not until 1981 that the entire collection was finally issued – on Granz's own Pablo label. The five discs constitute a remarkable document. For much of the time Lester actually plays better even than he does on the two sessions with Wilson and co. His sound, especially, is noticeably smoother and firmer, although he was presumably still using the plastic reed. It is possible that his saxophone had recently been overhauled. There are certainly none of the vanishing low notes, such as occur on *Jazz Giants '56* and which are commonly the result of leaking pads. Whatever the case, there are so many beautiful performances on the Washington discs that it is difficult to select a few outstanding examples, and the task is further complicated by the fact many tunes occur two or three times. There is nothing to choose, for instance, between the two versions each of 'Three Little Words', 'When You're Smiling' and 'Pennies From Heaven', all of which find Lester in positively exuberant spirits. When he is in a mood like this, with his powers of invention at full stretch, the weaknesses and fallings-off of recent times simply vanish. His tone is firm, his technique supple, even his breathing seems stronger. The tribulation and struggles of recent years have not, after all, extinguished the spark. And when we come to the ballads – 'These Foolish Things', 'I'm Confessin'', 'I Can't Get Started' – their cool, measured gravity is deeply moving.

A contributory factor to the success of the Washington week must surely have been the happy off-stage relationship between Lester and the Bill Potts trio. His caution in the presence of strangers, especially white strangers, seems to have been overcome instantly. There is certainly no suggestion of it in Potts's account:

> I can honestly say that never in my life have I met a more sincere, understanding, considerate, kind and sweet man...We had our own band room upstairs and, during intermissions, the four of us would just hang out. Willie, Jim and I would spend most of the time picking Lester's brains, as well as listening to some great stories of the old days. He was such a nice man, with a great sense of humour, and never said anything unkind about anyone.[11]

Who can resist hero worship? We know that Lester often felt unappreciated ('nobody likes old Prez') and the frank adoration of Bill Potts,

Norman 'Willie' Williams and Jim Lucht must have made him feel a lot better. That sense of well-being was instantly reflected in his performance, and the same process appears to have been at work the previous month, during the European tour with the Birdland Show. Whenever he had the chance he would jam with local musicians after the show, and a recording made at one such session, in Frankfurt, has a very similar, happy feeling. Indeed, appreciation appeared finally to be arriving from all quarters. Towards the end of the year, he was presented with a copy of Leonard Feather's *Encyclopedia Yearbook of Jazz*, inscribed with a flattering dedication declaring that a hundred fellow musicians had voted him the 'greatest-ever tenor saxophone'. It would have been nice if some of them had expressed their admiration a little earlier, and in person. To complete a remarkably good year, Mary gave birth to a daughter on New Year's Eve. They named her Yvette.

12 'let's review the books'

From time to time, throughout the 1950s, Lester appeared as guest soloist with Count Basie's band. It was now a very different band from the one he had been a member of, but he always enjoyed the experience. Various recordings survive, most of them rather scrappy affairs taken from live broadcasts, but the one made at the 1957 Newport Jazz Festival is much better. The date was 7 July, and there was a down-Memory-Lane flavour about the whole set, with Jo Jones and Jimmy Rushing also taking part. Lester plays his own two feature numbers, 'Polka Dots And Moonbeams' and 'Lester Leaps In', for which Basie carried fully prepared arrangements, and is then joined by Jones and Rushing for off-the-cuff versions of 'Sent For You Yesterday', 'Boogie Woogie' and 'Evenin''. His playing is remarkably forceful throughout and he improvises delightful accompanying lines behind Rushing.

In the up-and-down progress of these years, the Newport appearance marks a definite up. But the downs were becoming more frequent and distressing. He suffered an epileptic fit during a gig at Small's Paradise, an episode which the management wrongly attributed to drink. Everyone knew about Prez's alcoholism, and the story did his already flaking reputation no good. It was at around this time that Coleman Hawkins remarked to fellow-saxophonist Bud Freeman, 'That Lester Young! How does he get away with it? He's stoned half the time, he's always late, and he can't play.'[1] It was a brutal way of putting it, but there was an uncomfortable degree of truth in what he said. Even so, when he wasn't totally befuddled, Lester was still capable of sharp witticisms and shrewd musical observation. Stan Getz delighted in recounting his favourite example of the former, which occurred aboard a tour bus in 1957. Sonny Stitt, a formidably accomplished but aggressively competitive saxophone virtuoso, began stomping up and down the aisle, blowing blindingly fast passages. Everyone studiously ignored him or pretended to be asleep. Finally, he arrived at the back seat, where Lester was reclining, his hat over his eyes. 'Hey Prez! How about that, huh?' he demanded. Lester peered up at him from beneath the hat. 'Very nice, Lady Stitt', he murmured. 'Now can you sing me a song?'[2]

His musical opinions and insights could be both firm and original, and took no account of fashion or any prevailing ideology. We have, for instance, already heard him on the importance of knowing the lyric of a song. In a 1958 interview with Chris Albertson[3] he managed once more to put the cat firmly among the pigeons. Albertson asked him if he had ever heard Bessie Smith in person. Yes, he said, he had. And could he think of any singer in 1958 who reminded him of Bessie? 'Yes,' said Lester. 'Kay Starr'. This was not the answer Albertson was expecting. Kay Starr was a white (part native-American, in fact) popular singer of the day, of whom jazz buffs took little account. Surely, Albertson suggested, someone like Dakota Staton might be closer. But Prez not only stuck to Kay Starr, he urged Albertson to listen to her carefully: 'Listen to her voice, and play one of Bessie's records. See if you hear something.' And, if we follow his advice, we discover that he was quite right. Kay Starr does on occasion sound quite uncannily like Bessie Smith. Listen to her 1953 hit, 'Half A Photograph' – in particular the final three notes – and 'see if you hear something'. In an interview Kay Starr gave some years later, it turned out that Bessie Smith had, indeed, been one of her early idols. Still on the subject of singers, Lester then goes on to deliver a ringing endorsement of Jo Stafford. Nonplussed, Albertson objects that Jo Stafford is not a jazz singer, but Lester brushes this aside: 'No, but I hear her voice and the sound and the way she puts her songs on.' And it is undoubtedly true that musicians had always been among Jo Stafford's biggest fans, for the flawless accuracy of her intonation as much as anything. Lester, with his love of songs and singers, would have known her recordings of pieces such as 'The Things We Did Last Summer' (1946) and 'The Gentleman Is A Dope' (1955).

He took part in two package tours in 1957, a Birdland Stars show in February/March and JATP in September/October, together with a number of solo appearances, some as far apart as Hollywood and Toronto. His health was deteriorating all the time. A Norman Granz studio session in Hollywood on 31 July proved an almost total disaster. Lester had got hold of a metal clarinet, like the one he used to play with Basie, and plays one number on it – a blues that Granz named 'St Tropez'. The clarinet is a tricky instrument, and he had hardly touched one in years, a fact that quickly becomes obvious on listening to the two takes of 'St Tropez', but he does manage to create a weird kind of beauty out of the gasps and wheezes which emerge. The rest of the session is very sad from his point of view. The slow 'I Cover The Waterfront' is just about passable, but the up-tempo 'Sunday' defeats him. Coleman Hawkins's brusque dismissal applies only too well in this case; he cannot, in any meaningful sense of the term, play at all. And yet this was only twenty-four days after the quite sparky and encouraging Newport set with Basie. Twenty-four days and around three thousand miles, if you include a trip to Chicago on the 13th. He had spent his entire life on the road, but he was in no state to keep up this kind of pace.

A major television showcase for jazz had been commissioned by the CBS network, to be transmitted on 8 December, with a huge cast, including Basie, Hawkins, Ben Webster, Gerry Mulligan, Vic Dickenson, Jo Jones and Billie Holiday. There were plans for Lester to play at several points, but when he showed up for rehearsal he was so weak and ill-looking that his participation was reduced to one solo in Billie's set. There had been rumours of a rift, or at least some coolness, between them, although no one seemed to know the reason. Lester always mentioned the name of Lady Day with affection, and Billie never said anything derogatory about him. However, in her autobiography she does say, 'You can hurt his feelings in two seconds. I know, because I found out once that I had'.[4] Whatever the case, it was all forgotten now. Lester's performance in the grainy, black-and-white film record is brief but desperately moving. He rises slowly from his chair, fixes Billie with sad, hooded eyes and plays a single, twelve-bar chorus of such purity and restraint that the despair contained within it shines like a cold moon through ragged clouds. She gazes back, smiling sadly.

Soon afterwards he was back in hospital. Among the various disorders from which he suffered were alcoholism and its attendant conditions, malnutrition and cirrhosis of the liver. Then there was the epilepsy and, to make matters worse, his teeth were in appalling condition. He was depressed and confused. And what of the syphilis, which had apparently been detected at his Army medical, back in 1944? In a rather indistinct taped conversation with writer and researcher Michael Brooks, John Hammond claimed that a number of Basie musicians had tested positive for syphilis years before, when Jo Jones had begun behaving oddly:

> When Jo Jones blew his top in Pittsburgh in 1937, I made the band have a venereal inspection...and Jo they found to have syphilis in the second degree. They found six guys in Basie's band who had the same thing (and of course that was in the days before penicillin) and Lester was one of the worst offenders in the band. And all during the time in the forties, you know, when he was acting strangely and everything, I used to tell Marshall Stearns...have you ever really checked on the venereal history of Lester Young, because, I said, I'm sure it's in the tertiary stage right now, but he never did.[5]

(It is likely that Hammond meant 'fifties', rather than 'forties'. Marshall Stearns was Professor of English at Hunter College and founder of the Institute of Jazz Studies. More about him below.)

Frank Büchmann-Møller examined the syphilis question in some detail in 1990,[6] taking as his starting point the fluctuations in Lester's performance and his decreasing instrumental agility during the late 1950s. There was also the curious gait, described by Bobby Scott as 'more a shuffle than an honest walk', which had also been remarked upon by others. One common symptom of syphilis is tabes dorsalis, or locomotor ataxia, a disorder of the spinal chord, which results in a shuffling gait, loss of sensation in the extremities and what might, in everyday English, be described as 'clumsiness'. Another common symptom is paresis, which brings depression, mood swings, insomnia and emotional instability in general. All this seems to fit, although it is by no means conclusive. Lester's daughter, Yvette, for instance, was born at the end of 1956, even though impotence is commonly associated with tertiary stage syphilis. Neither did Mary contract the disease, nor was it passed on to either of their children.

If he did have syphilis, and knew he had it, and realized that his declining powers were the result of having it, then he would have known that the outlook was hopeless. He would also have been in permanent pain of one kind or another, which alcohol helped to alleviate. The choice, in such a case, was between increasing pain, coupled with constant awareness of his advancing disease, on the one hand, and drinking himself to death, on the other. Either way, he was bound to die soon. Viewed in the light of this predicament, his next decision makes some kind of sense. In the spring of 1958, he left Mary and the children and the house in St Albans and moved into the Alvin, a cheap hotel on the corner of Broadway and 52nd Street, overlooking Birdland. The reason he gave Mary was that he needed to be closer to the centre of things, and that's the story which she loyally passed on to the rest of the world. 'It wasn't that the marriage ever really broke up,' she told Leonard Feather. 'He just wanted to be in New York where things were happening.'[7] But could it have been that he did not want to do his dying in the bosom of his family? He couldn't run away from trouble this time, but he could remove himself and his distress from their presence. It is at least a possibility.

Soon after his release from Kings County Hospital, and not long before moving to the Alvin, Lester recorded two studio sessions for Granz, on 7 and 8 February. There are some unbearably moving passages, particularly in both takes of 'You're Getting To Be A Habit With Me', although you need to be acquainted with the circumstances to appreciate them fully. They amount to a distillation of pain and despair and one does not confront them easily. In 'They Can't Take That Away From Me', Lester plays an opening clarinet chorus which, rather like his wraith-like tenor solo in the *Sound of Jazz* show, is a triumph of spirit against the odds. Some notes are half-voiced, and some fail to escape from the instrument at all, but as a paraphrase of George Gershwin's tune it is a masterpiece, and quintessential Lester Young – careful, probing, rhythmically elusive and wickedly devious. It is his last great utterance. The album containing it was entitled, significantly, *Laughin' To Keep From Cryin'*. People who knew him at this time, and were only too aware of his failing condition, sometimes remarked on Lester's continued ability to laugh and joke among friends, and the cover of the album catches this in a wonderful photograph. It shows Roy Eldridge and Lester sitting together at the session. Eldridge is obviously telling a joke and Lester is laughing so hard that he seems in imminent danger of falling off his chair. It must have been at around the same time, too, that Jo Jones encountered Lester shuffling down the street, pushing the infant Yvette in her baby-carriage. How was he coping in the role of father, in particular with the child's excretory functions? 'Well,' replied Lester, 'I don't mind the waterfall, but I can't stand the mustard!'[8]

Once ensconced in the Alvin, however, he grew increasingly remote. He would sit staring out of the window at Birdland opposite, watching the musicians as they turned up to work, drinking steadily, eating nothing. In the background the phonograph played on and on – Sinatra, Dick Haymes, Jo Stafford, Lady Day – songs with words. From time to time he would visit one of the cheap, triple-bill movie houses on 42nd Street. Westerns were his favourite. He was joined at the Alvin by Elaine Swain, a young woman who had lived with several other musicians and was, apparently, a devoted companion. She took care of him as well as she could and spent hours listening to him talk, recording his rambling discourse in a series of notebooks, which she allowed no one else to read. Everyone knew of Lester's plight but nobody knew what might be done about it. Visitors were not discouraged, but personal questions were turned aside and offers of help ignored. The hotel bill was discreetly settled by friends, the great drummer Max Roach among them. Marshall Stearns paid a visit and was appalled at what he found. He realized that nothing could be done without Lester's co-operation, and that meant getting through his elaborate defence system, in particular his distrust of doctors. Fortunately, Stearns knew someone who might be able to manage it, a jazz-loving psychiatrist and physician with the improbable name of Dr Luther Cloud.

Concealing his professional interest, Cloud began calling on Lester to talk about music and listen to tales of the old days.

> It may have been three or four visits, I can't recall exactly, before I said to him, 'Lester, you know I do admire your music, no doubt about it, but I have to be straight with you. I also happen to be a practising physician and I think you need some help.' He accepted it beautifully, although he wouldn't have accepted it the first time around. I worked with him closely for those last two years of his life. For most of those two years he was able to moderate his behaviour, contain it quite well, not drink daily and, when he did drink, maybe a little wine or something like that.[9]

Cloud got him to eat a little and to take vitamin pills. He also wanted to give him some injections, but Lester baulked at that. Slowly, some of his strength returned. 'In six months,' Cloud recalled, 'he had added weight, was talking sense, dressing and going outdoors.'[10] And the improvement rekindled his desire to play.

Figure 14. 1958. Weary but still trying. Dickie Wells took this slightly wonky but touching snapshot of Prez during the set-up for the iconic Esquire photo of fifty-seven jazz greats in Harlem. (Frank Driggs collection)

The problem now was that Charlie Carpenter had given up on him, as had the Moe Gale agency, and he was in no condition to embark on a tour. Then Marshall Stearns had an idea for gently relaunching his career. Lester had left his father's band and joined Art Bronson's Bostonians in 1928, so one could plausibly claim that 1958 was his thirtieth year as a professional musician. Stearns suggested a special 'Thirty Years in Show Business' celebration gig at Birdland, to which Lester agreed enthusiastically. Stearns also undertook to talk to Oscar Goldstein, Birdland's manager, and negotiate a hundred-dollar fee on Lester's behalf. Goldstein agreed to the show readily enough, but refused to budge from his standard fifty-dollar nightly rate for headline artists. Stearns himself made up the difference.

The show took place on 2 June and was a great success. The club was full and Lester played three sets. After a shaky start, according to reports in the music press, he played very well and was warmly received. During one intermission, a cake with candles was brought out, a event which was greeted by Lester playing the opening bars of 'I Didn't Know What Time It Was', to general laughter and applause. The evening served its purpose in announcing to the world that Prez was back in business, and the gigs began coming in, beginning with three further weeks at Birdland. To those who had seen him only a month or two earlier, the change was next to miraculous. But his health and spirits were still in a precarious state. It took only one small setback to plunge him back into despair, and that came at the Newport Jazz Festival in July. He found himself placed in a scratch, mainstream-cum-Dixieland group with Jack Teagarden, Pee Wee Russell, Jo Jones, Buck Clayton and others. None of them seemed overjoyed with the arrangement, and early in the set it came on to rain, casting a further pall over the proceedings. A gloomy Lester shared the return journey to New York in the back of a car with Buddy Tate:

> 'Give me a cigarette,' he says. 'Let's review the books.' And we started talking about through the years and he told me about his ups and downs...
>
> And he says, 'You know, I never really made it on my own.'
>
> I says, 'You've gotta be kidding!... Prez, everybody in the world knows you, Coleman Hawkins and Louis Armstrong.'
>
> And he says, 'Yeah, but all the other ladies [are] makin' all the money.'
>
> He was very unhappy. Very, very unhappy.[11]

This up-and-down pattern was repeated throughout the rest of 1958. Most of his work was around the New York–Newark area, with a couple of trips to Philadelphia and one to Chicago. His main New York base was the Five Spot Café, at Cooper Square, just off the Bowery. The 1959 *Metronome Year Book* carried a 'photographic essay' by Herb Snitzer, who shadowed Prez over the course of an evening at the Five Spot and captured very well the atmosphere of a night's work – the backstage conversation, the small, dimly lit room, the complete lack of show business pretension in the whole affair. It was the ambiance in which he always felt most comfortable. The final frame shows Lester on his way home to the Alvin, dropping his token into the entrance gate at a subway station.

And so he might have continued, shambling on into an indefinite future, his health moderately stable under the watchful care of Elaine Swain, Dr Cloud, Marshall Stearns and others, and his spirits buoyed up by friends like Buddy Tate and Willie Jones. But then came the offer of an eight-week engagement in Paris, at the Blue Note club, after which it was planned that he would join up with a JATP European tour, scheduled to open in Paris. This was a hazardous undertaking. He would have to fly to Paris alone, and live there for two months without his friends and supporters. One of the great might-have-beens of jazz is the question: what would have happened if the French offer had never been made? But the offer did come, and it could not be refused. Quite apart from the money, there was the boost to his self-esteem. Prez was an artist of international stature once more, and he was looking forward to the trip. He went out to St Albans, to say goodbye to Mary, Little Lester and baby Yvette, and received a visit at the Alvin from his brother, Lee. Better qualified than anyone to know Lester's character, Lee had serious misgivings about the whole enterprise: 'He was not a good business man, you know...and they could take advantage of him from every angle you could think of.'[12]

Lester flew to Paris on or about 20 January 1959. Elaine Swain went with him to the airport. On arrival in Paris he was met and checked in at the Hôtel de la Louisiane, in Rue de Seine. Calling at the Blue Note on the 22nd, the night before he was due to open, he met Stan Getz, whose engagement there was just ending. Fixing Getz with a steady gaze he smiled and said, 'Lady Getz, you're my singer.' Getz treasured this as a second benediction. They would never meet again. Lester had already made a few friends in Paris during his JATP visits. Notable among these was Maurice Cullaz, a great jazz lover, and his wife, Yvonne, whom Lester called 'Lady Queen'. According to a sad, affectionate memoir which Cullaz wrote after Lester's death, Lester confided to him that he expected to die soon, and had even begun referring to himself in the past tense.[13] But he settled down to play the engagement with all the determination he could muster. His accompanists were pianist René Urtreger, Pierre Michelot on bass, Kenny Clarke, the pioneer bebop drummer, now resident in Paris, and guitarist Jimmy Gourley, another American expatriate. It was a strong team and all went well for the first couple of weeks, until Urtreger and Michelot had to leave for another engagement. Their replacements were adequate, but the difference was marked and Prez felt it keenly. Before long, in the absence of his support network, he began drinking again. He telephoned Dr Cloud a few times and admitted as much:

> He would pick up the phone and call, maybe three times in about three weeks, and he was very honest with me. He told me he was drinking, and he was drinking absinthe, which you can't get in this country, which is very high-potency and very toxic, even to a non-alcoholic. He was little unhappy, after a while, with the gigs he was doing. He didn't feel that his supporting cast was up to his calibre... But I think also he was losing his own discernment. He was drinking heavily.[14]

It was on 6 February, in the third week of his Blue Note residency, that Lester recorded his now-famous interview with the French journalist François Postif. It is his longest and most oft-quoted (indeed, it has frequently been quoted in the course of this present narrative), but it was conducted when he was ill, depressed, disorientated and drunk. Parts of it are soggy and virtually incomprehensible, even by Prez's elliptical standards. Most of it is a run-through of his life-story, with the emphasis on incidents which continued to obsess him, such as being suspended from the family band and the episode with 'that bitch, Henderson's wife'. He tells how he came to switch from alto to tenor saxophone in Art Bronson's Bostonians and how he invited himself back into Basie's band after hearing it on the radio. As usual, he evades the question of how he came to leave it in December 1940. He also claims to be 'feeling a draft', which is surprising, since Paris in the 1950s was generally regarded as one of the least racist of cities. As with his playing, so with his discourse, one must always be prepared for the occasional dazzling insight, obliquely but acutely expressed, and there is one beauty here: 'They want everybody who's a Negro to be an Uncle Tom, or Uncle Remus, or Uncle Sam – and I can't make it!' He had never been submissive (Uncle Tom), nor lovably garrulous (Uncle Remus), and the US Army had cause to know exactly what he thought of Uncle Sam.

His gloom was lightened somewhat when Billie Holiday came to Paris, to appear at the Mars Club and give a concert at L'Olympia. He also acquired a female companion, a young German woman, whom he called 'Miss Wiggins'. The novelist James Jones (author of *From Here to Eternity*), recalled meeting him in Paris on several occasions and summed up his demeanour in two poignantly exact words, 'princely helplessness'.[15]

On 2 March 1959 Lester made what turned out to be his last recording session, with Urtreger and company at the Barclay studios in Paris. It marks a dismal end to a recording career of such profound importance in the history of jazz music. He sounds weaker than ever. His shortness of breath will not permit phrases lasting longer than about five seconds and his embouchure wavers on even moderately sustained notes. It is simply heartbreaking to hear him struggle through (of all things) 'Lady Be Good', one of the pieces with which he announced his arrival at his very first recording session in 1936. Listening to the two performances, one after the other, is to hear two players who are complete strangers to one another. The first is an energetic young man who, like most young people, assumes himself to be immortal. The second is a sick, prematurely aged man who knows he is dying. The first produces musical statements of formidable power, fluency and wit. The second utters mere contingent fragments. Nothing connects with anything else. Strength has departed from lungs and fingers. Mind is at the end of its tether. Spirit is slipping away.

He managed to get through to the end of the seventh week, but was then too ill to continue. He was suffering severe pains in his stomach and was almost too weak to get out of bed. He did not want to see a French doctor or to go to hospital, he said. All he wanted was to go home. He played his last set at the Blue Note on Friday 13 March. The following day he gathered his few belongings together, someone fixed his air ticket and took him to Orly airport. By the time his plane took off the pains were almost unbearable, and soon he began vomiting blood. The cause was varicose veins attached to his oesophagus; these had ruptured and were bleeding internally. In 1959 a westbound trans-Atlantic flight took at least eight-and-a-half hours and Lester, imprisoned in his seat, bled and suffered all the way. The pain was so severe that he bit through his upper lip, causing more bleeding.

There is some doubt as to whether Elaine Swain met him at Idlewild (now JFK) airport. Whatever the case, he went straight back to his room at the Alvin and his chair by the window, drinking steadily between bouts of sickness. Eventually, as the Broadway lights blinked on, he lay down on the bed and seemed to fall asleep. At around one o'clock on the morning of 15 March he awoke in a drunken stupor, began feebly moving his fingers and seemed to be trying to form his lips into an embouchure. Elaine called for help. A doctor arrived soon afterwards, but could do nothing. Lester died at three o'clock. He was aged forty-nine years, six months and sixteen days.

Such was the confusion surrounding the death – a cheap hotel room, a corpse with a bloodied face, a frightened young woman – that the police were called. They impounded everything of obvious value, including Lester's gold ring, his passport, his wallet containing $500 in traveller's cheques and his voice, a well-worn and much-repaired Conn 10M tenor saxophone in a scuffed leather case. Once the cause of death had been established these were passed on to Mary.

When great men die, people remember where they were when they heard the news. Jo Jones was at home, reading the sports page of the paper he had bought in the street outside the Alvin Hotel as Lester was sinking into his final stupor. Dr Cloud was driving home from New Jersey and heard it on his car radio. In places far remote from New York City, musicians and lovers of jazz learned of the death without surprise but with a sense of infinite loss. They had followed the faltering tale of the past few years, chronicled in recordings which recounted it all too clearly. He had called it 'telling your story', and he had told his story with such honesty and candour that even the worst parts were plain for all to hear. A lesser man might have dissembled, put on an act, but to lie was not in his nature. Lester Young's art is entirely true to itself. Therein lies its tragedy.

The funeral was a decent, well-conducted affair. Lee, Beverly, Mary, Little Lester – all the scattered family, including Lizetta, mourning the death of her firstborn, gathered at Universal Chapel on 52nd Street and Lexington Avenue on 19 March. Jo Jones, Jimmy Rushing, Dickie Wells, Buddy Tate and dozens more of Prez's contemporaries and friends were there. Mrs Catherine Basie took the place of her husband, who was on tour in California. Billie Holiday arrived, wanting to sing, but Mary, seeing the state she was in, wouldn't allow it. Billie herself was to die within four months. Al Hibbler sang 'In The Garden', a song he had composed for the occasion, and trombonist Tyree Glenn played 'Just A'Wearyin' For You', a beautiful old melody by Carrie Jacobs Bond which Prez had loved. Tributes appeared in the papers. Record companies began sifting through their back-catalogues with memorial albums in mind. (Lester had predicted that they would.) He lies buried at Evergreen Cemetery, in the New York Borough of Queens.

13 'ivey-divey!'

Reading through interviews with Lester Young, the recollections of his friends and stray remarks of his that were picked up and quoted, one notices a recurrent theme. He was constantly protesting that he minded his own business and didn't bother anyone. His aim at such moments seemed to be to pass through the world causing as little disturbance as possible. In this, despite his best efforts, he failed. If, as humanists assert, our personalities survive in the memories of other people, in the work we do, the emotions we stir and the effect we have on the world in general, then we must conclude that he is still very much with us.

Consider the image of Prez in *Jammin' The Blues*, deep in a midnight world of his own, blowing for himself amidst the drifting smoke. Like Bogart glimpsed through the raindrops on a windshield, the picture has become a symbol, powerfully evoking a time, a place and an attitude to life. And, like the Bogart picture, it inspired emulation. There were people who wanted to be just like that – cool, detached, undemonstratively eloquent. It comes as no surprise to find, a few years later, the name of Lester Young among the founding deities of the Beat Generation. Allen Ginsberg claimed that his archetypal Beat poem, 'Howl', was inspired by 'Lester Leaps In'.[1] References to Lester occur throughout the work of Jack Kerouac, while Edgar Pool, the principal character in John Clellon Holmes's novel, *The Horn* (1953), is a kind of amalgam of Lester and Charlie Parker. In later years, the mere mention of a Lester Young record became useful shorthand for a *film noir*, low-life setting in novels by Chester Himes, Elmore Leonard *et al.* In Peter Straub's *Pork Pie Hat* (1999), the narrator meets a Prez-like figure, dying of alcoholism, who tells tales from a mysterious past. Perhaps inevitably, Lester came to be classed along with Parker as a prime example of the doomed, self-destructive artist. Edgar Pool is the classic outsider, a man 'self-damned to difference'. In Bertrand Tavernier's film *Round Midnight* (1986), Dale Turner, a combination of Prez and Bud Powell, played by Dexter Gordon, struggles to straighten out his life but loses his precarious balance and is destroyed.

That is one form of immortality, to offer a pattern for other people's imaginings, but there are more. For instance, we also survive through our genes, and even Prez, who had seen most things, would have been momentarily astonished if he could have foreseen how his son was to turn out. Because Little Lester became everything that his father wasn't, and everything that his grandfather would have wished. The following extract from a 2003 press release, issued by the Institute for Student Achievement in New York, will serve to illustrate: 'Dr Lester Young Jnr, Superintendent of Community School District 13 in Brooklyn, has been appointed by Mayor Bloomberg to head up the NYC Department of Education's newly redesigned Office of Youth Development and School-Community Services... Under Dr Young's leadership, the office will work to ensure that students receive the effective health, mental health, guidance and educational enrichment services necessary to create and sustain academic achievement...' And so on, for a further two-and-a-half worthy paragraphs. As Prez himself might have commented, 'Ivey-divey!'

And what of his disciples, the followers whose devotion had caused him so much anguish? Although he complained about 'copycats' in a general way, he never accused anyone in particular of being one. Neither could he help admiring someone as accomplished and eloquent as Stan Getz, 'my singer'. Towards the end of his life, for instance during that last, long conversation in the car with Buddy Tate, he did grumble that 'all the other ladies [are] making all the money', but that was in the context of his own distress and self-accusation. Several writers, Prof. Daniels among them, speak as though it were a simple matter of white imitators copying a few Lester Young licks and making off with the cash. This is a vulgar travesty. Lester Young was a major artist, and major artists almost inevitably become major influences. In English poetry, look at Milton, or Wordsworth, or Eliot. In jazz, look at Armstrong. Look at Hawkins. Look at Parker. Their magnetic fields were, for a while, inescapable, but the best disciples absorbed their lessons and developed their own musical personalities. Charlie Parker himself was strongly influenced by Lester Young, as his earliest recordings plainly reveal. Lester's light, floating tone, the clear, uninsistent line, the rhythmic subtlety – all these characteristics can be traced through several later generations of tenor saxophonists, but rarely does one come across a case of direct imitation after about 1950.[2] The point about the twin influences of Lester Young and bebop on tenor saxophone style has already been made. With the rise to prominence of Sonny Rollins and John Coltrane, Lester's influence became less marked, but it is unmistakably present in the round tone and cool, balanced phrasing of their contemporary, Hank Mobley. In more recent times, the advent of 'neo-classical' players such as Scott Hamilton and Harry Allen has maintained that thread of influence.

At a more profound level, a case can be made for Lester's importance as a seminal influence on Miles Davis, and thus on the emergence of 'modal' improvisation in the 1960s, and all that followed from it. There was a great and well-documented mutual admiration between Lester and Miles.[3] In his autobiography, Miles claims that he learned from Lester the 'running style of playing' which has a 'softness in the approach and concept and places emphasis on one note'.[4] He contrasts this with the bebop of Parker and Gillespie, whose approach was 'more rather than less', and who used 'a lot of real fast notes and chord changes'. He on the other hand was seeking the opposite, 'a kind of stretched-out sound'. Lester's reluctance to chase after complex, chromatic chord patterns, but instead to find a way through them which emphasized melodic line, has already been noted. His recordings with John Lewis in particular owe much of their charm to this very tendency. His ear, as Gunther Schuller points out, was essentially diatonic. His 'emphasis on both the melodic use of fourth and fifth intervals and harmonically on the sixth and ninth steps of the scale, combined with his linear conception of phrasing'[5] led eventually to the 'kind of stretched-out sound', the less-is-more approach which Miles Davis had been seeking. He finally realized it in *Kind Of Blue*, his album which became the decisive exemplar of modal improvisation. Its recording coincided almost exactly with Lester Young's death. It was made between March and April 1959. Lester died on 15 March.

But granted his importance as an artistic influence, a sub-cultural icon, the source of oft-quoted jazz anecdotes and the originator of a personal vocabulary, several terms from which have passed into common parlance – over and above all these, Lester Young remains with us because of the music he recorded. Fortunately, there is a great deal of it – studio sessions with Basie (both big band and small groups), with Billie Holiday, with his own band, with ad hoc bands, bands made up of JATP members, live recordings (both official and unofficial), broadcasts, television and film soundtracks, rehearsals. In the years since his death they have appeared fitfully in whatever the current medium happened to be – EP, ten-inch LP, twelve-inch LP, various kinds of tape, CD, MP3. They have come as single discs, gatefold albums and boxed sets, emanating from multi-national corporations or from obscure outfits based in tiny principalities where the laws of copyright appear to be unknown. One could be churlish and say that, to all of them, Lester Young is worth more dead than he ever was alive.

And yet, one has only to listen to a few bars from any of this tottering pile of material to be captivated. Whether he is bursting joyously loose from the choreography of the Basie ensemble, conducting one of his half-loving, half-kidding conversations with Lady Day, or deftly turning a familiar melody into something distinctively his own, there is never any doubt that this is purposeful, immediate, constantly surprising, serious music, and its seriousness is self-evident. As Philip Larkin put it, 'Nobody had to tell you; he told you himself'.[6] The beauty of Lester Young's music endures. Even in its worst moments, when mere execution seems a near-insuperable problem, its very fragility conveys a unique essence. If there is a word to describe it, that word is 'truth'.

notes

Sources most frequently quoted

DB   *Down Beat*

DHD   Douglas Henry Daniels, *Lester Leaps In* (Boston: Beacon Press, 1990)

FB-M   Frank Büchmann-Møller, *You Just Fight for Your Life* (New York: Praeger, 1990)

FP   François Postif, interview with Lester Young, *Jazz Hot* 142 (April 1959)

LYR   Lewis Porter, ed., *A Lester Young Reader* (Washington, DC: Smithsonian Institution Press, 1991)

MM   *Melody Maker*

Chapter 1

1 FP.

2 Danny Barker, quoted in *Hear Me Talkin' To Ya* (New York: Rinehart, 1955), ed. Nat Shapiro and Nat Hentoff, p. 3.

3 FP.

4 Interview with Leonard Feather, MM, 15 July 1950.

5 DHD, p. 40.

6 FP.

7 John Wesley Work Jnr, *American Negro Songs* (1940), quoted by Dan Morgenstern in notes to album *Ma Rainey* (Milestone M-47021).

8 Leonard Phillips, interviewed for Rutgers Jazz Oral History Project, Institute of Jazz Studies, Rutgers University, Newark, New Jersey, January 1983, quoted in FB-M.

9 FP.

10 DHD, p. 42.

11 Interview for Rutgers Jazz Oral History Project. Transcription published in LYR, pp. 21-22.

12 See note 8.

13 Interview for Rutgers Jazz Oral History Project, quoted in FB-M, p. 24.

14 Nat Shapiro and Nat Hentoff, *The Jazz Makers* (London: Peter Davies, 1958), p. 246.

15 FP.

16 Mitzy Trumbauer, quoted in album notes to *Lester Young Story Vol. 1* (CBS 88223) by Michael Brooks, 1976.

17 Interview with Pat Harris, DB, 6 May 1949.

18 See note 8.

19 Ibid.

Chapter 2

1 Leonard Phillips, Rutgers Jazz Oral History Project, quoted in FB-M, p. 29.

2 FP.

3 Interview, *Jazz Record*, July 1946.

4 Eddie Barefield, Rutgers Jazz Oral History Project, quoted in FB-M, p. 31.

5 Ross Russell, *Jazz Style in Kansas City and the South-West* (Berkeley, CA: University of California Press, 1971), p. 80.

6 Buster Smith interview, DB, 11 July 1956.

7 Interview, MM, 15 July 1950. (The term 'every tub' is a contraction of the proverbial expression 'every tub on its own bottom'. A few years later, one of Lester's feature numbers with Count Basie's orchestra was entitled *Every Tub*.)

8 Leonard Phillips, Rutgers Jazz Oral History Project, quoted in FB-M, p. 38.

10 Interview, DB, 7 March 1956.

11 Ralph Ellison, *Shadow and Act* (New York: Vintage Books, 1964), pp. 236-37.

12 Interview with Russell Davies, 1981 (tape, private collection).

13 For more on this topic, see chapter on Lester Young in Gunther Schuller, *The Swing Era* (New York: Oxford University Press, 1989).

14 Maurice M. Milligan, *The Inside Story of the Pendergast Machine by the Man Who Smashed It* (New York: Charles Scribner's Sons, 1948), pp. 11-12.

15 Ibid., p. 84.

16 Ibid., p. 84.

17 Nathan W. Pearson, *Goin' to Kansas City* (Urbana IL: University of Illinois Press, 1987), p. 121.

18 Shapiro and Hentoff, *The Jazz Makers*, p. 250.

19 FP.

20 MM, 'Battle of the Tenor Kings', 1 May 1954, p. 11.

21 Dempsey Travis, *Autobiography of Black Jazz* (Chicago: Urban Research Institute, 1984), p. 296.

22 John Hammond interview with Michael Brooks, 1974 (tape, private collection).

23 Brian Case, 'Buddy Tate and the President', MM, 1 December 1979.

24 MM, 6 June 1934.

25 'Hocus Pocus' / 'Phantom Fantasie' / 'Harlem Madness' / 'Tidal Wave', by Fletcher Henderson and his Orchestra, Victor Records, New York City, 6 March 1934.

26 See note 22.

27 Shapiro and Hentoff, *The Jazz Makers*, p. 250.

28 Billie Holiday, *Lady Sings the Blues* (Garden City, NY: Doubleday, 1956), p. 56.

29 Ibid., p. 49.

30 FP.

31 Buddy Tate, interview with Russell Davies, 1981 (tape, private collection).

32 Interview, DB, 7 March 1956.

Chapter 3

1 Count Basie with Albert Murray, *Good Morning Blues* (London: Heinemann, 1986), p. 157.

2 Ibid., p. 161.

3 John Hammond and Irving Townsend, *John Hammond on Record* (Harmondsworth: Penguin Books, 1981), p. 165.

4 Basie, *Good Morning Blues*, p. 167.

5 Hammond and Townsend, *John Hammond on Record*, pp. 170-71.

6 John Hammond, 'Recollections', *Jazz & Blues*, August 1973, p. 9.

7 Basie, *Good Morning Blues*, p. 180.

8 *Metronome* magazine, 'Pick-up' column, January 1937, p. 26.

9 Interview with Russell Davies, 1981 (tape, private collection).

10 Both 'Shoe Shine Boy' and 'Lady Be Good' have been the subject of sustained and repeated musical analysis. The most exhaustive examination of the former, by Lawrence Gushee, originally delivered as a paper to the International Musicological Society, appears in LYR (pp. 224-54). A close exegesis of the latter can be found in Schuller, *The Swing Era*, pp. 230-35.

Chapter 4

1   Count Basie, *Good Morning Blues*, p. 185.
2   Ibid., p. 187.
3   Interview with Pat Harris, DB, 6 May 1949.
4   Dickie Wells, *The Night People* (Boston: Crescendo Publishing, 1971), p. 55.
5   Hammond and Townsend, *John Hammond on Record*, p. 148.
6   Count Basie, *Good Morning Blues*, p. 188.
7   http://us.imdb.com
8   Unpublished interview with Stan Britt, c. 1980.
9   Leonard Feather, *From Satchmo to Miles* (New York: Da Capo Press, 1984), p. 121.
10 Ross Russell, 'Bebop', in *The Art of Jazz*, ed. Martin Williams (New York: Oxford University Press, 1959), p. 212.
11 This can be teased out thus: Bing Crosby, the popular singer, and his brother, Bob Crosby, the bandleader, were of Irish extraction, as was a large contingent of the New York Police Department.

Chapter 5

1   Billie Holiday, *Hear Me Talkin' To Ya*, p. 310.
2   Conversation with author, 1995.
3   Billie Holiday, *Lady Sings The Blues*, p. 58.
4   Interview with Gary Giddins for Rutgers Jazz Oral History Project, quoted by FB-M, p. 88.
5   Ibid.
6   DB, 15 October 1939.

Chapter 6

1   FP.
2   DHD, p. 234.
3   Interview, BBC Radio 2, c. 1982.
4   Quoted in Donald Clarke, *Wishing on the Moon* (London: Viking Press, 1994), p. 126.
5   Quoted in Gene Lees, *Oscar Peterson: The Will to Swing* (London: Macmillan, 1989), p. 89.
6   Ibid.
7   In conversation with author, February 1988.
8   Gene Lees, *The Singer and the Song* (New York: Oxford University Press, 1987), p. 92.

Chapter 7

1 Rutgers Jazz Oral History Project, quoted in FB-M, p. 111.
2 Count Basie, *Good Morning Blues*, p. 264.
3 Whitney Balliett, *American Musicians: 56 Portraits in Jazz* (New York: Oxford University Press, 1986), p. 264.
4 Ibid.
5 Ibid.
6 DB, 1 December 1944.

Chapter 8

1 Interview with Brian Case, MM, 1 December 1979.
2 Ibid.
3 Lee Young interviewed by Patricia Willard for Rutgers Jazz Oral History Project, quoted in FB-M, p. 118.
4 Ulysses Lee, *The US Army in World War II: Employment of Negro Troops* (US Govt. Printing Service, Washington DC, 1966).

Chapter 9

1 Ross Russell, *Bird Lives* (London: Quartet Books, 1972); see chapter 'The Independent Record Derby', p. 191 ff.
2 'Back To The Land', 'I Cover The Waterfront', 'Somebody Loves Me', 'I've Found A New Baby', 'The Man I Love', 'Peg O' My Heart', 'I Want To Be Happy', 'Mean To Me'.
3 'You're Driving Me Crazy', 'New Lester Leaps In, 'Lester's Bebop Boogie', 'She's Funny That Way'.
4 FB-M, p. 149.

Chapter 10

1 Leonard Feather, *Satchmo to Miles* (London: Quartet Books, 1972), p. 119.
2 Interview with Bob Rusch, *Cadence* magazine 10.3 (1984).
3 DB, 10 March 1948.
4 DB, 3 December 1947.
5 Leonard Feather notes to Blue Note CD edition of the complete Aladdin recordings.
6 'Tea For Two', 'East Of The Sun', 'The Sheik Of Araby', 'Something To Remember You By' (28 December 1948).
7 Interview with Chris Albertson c. 1958, in *The World of Count Basie*, ed. Stanley Dance (London: Sidgwick & Jackson, 1980), p. 31.

8   FP.

9   Interview with Pat Harris, DB, 6 May 1949.

10 Interview with Allan Morrison, *Jazz Record*, July 1946.

11 Max Roach, quoted in FB-M, p. 158.

12 DB, 7 March 1956.

13 Bobby Scott, 'The House in the Heart', *Gene Lees Jazzletter*, September 1983, reprinted in LYR, pp. 99–118.

14 FB-M, p. 149.

15 June 1950, 16 January 1951, 8 March 1951.

16 Graham Colombé, 'Presidents Ain't What They Used To Be', *Into Jazz* magazine, London, April 1974.

17 'Too Marvellous For Words' (Frankie Laine, 1951); 'It All Depends On You' (Frank Sinatra, 1949): 'Count Every Star' (Dick Haymes, 1950); 'Thou Swell' (Bing Crosby, 1951); 'Three Little Words' (Rudy Vallee, 1950); ''Deed I Do' (Lena Horne, 1948).

18 Interview with Nat Hentoff, DB, 7 March 1956.

19 Shapiro and Hentoff, *The Jazz Makers*, p. 265.

20 Ibid.

21 MM, 21 March 1953.

22 Contained in Complete Lester Young Verve Studio Sessions (Verve 314 547 087-2.

23 As in the old New Orleans street song, 'Funky butt, funky butt, take it away!'

24 MM, 21 March 1953.

25 Much-repeated Ronnie Scott anecdote.

Chapter 11

1   Max Jones, *Talking Jazz* (London: Macmillan Press, 1988), p. 52.

2   MM, 15 July 1950.

3   WNEW *Saturday Night Swing Session*, 12 April 1947 (Counterpoint CPT 549).

4   Nat Hentoff, DB, 7 March 1956.

5   Bobby Scott, 'The House in the Heart', *Gene Lees Jazzletter*, September 1983, reprinted in LYR, pp. 99–118.

6   Ibid.

7   'A Prisoner Of Love', 'Taking A Chance On Love', 'All Of Me', 'Louise', 'Our Love Is Here To Stay', 'Love Me Or Leave Me'.

8   Bobby Scott, *op. cit.*

9   FB-M, p. 193.

10 Bill Potts, notes to CD *Lester Young In Washington 1956, Vol. 1* (Pablo OJCCD 782-2).

11 Ibid.

Chapter 12

1   In Bud Freeman's autobiography, *You Don't Look Like a Musician* (Detroit: Balamp Publishing, 1974), p. 101.

2   Stan Getz, in conversation with author, 1986.

3   Transcribed in LYR, pp. 165-72.

4   Billie Holiday, *Lady Sings The Blues*, p. 58.

5   John Hammond, taped interview with Michael Brooks, c. 1974 (private collection).

6   'The Last Years of Lester Young', *Jazz Times*, September 1990, reprinted in LYR, pp. 122-25.

7   Leonard Feather, *From Satchmo To Miles* (London: Quartet Books, 1972), p. 125.

8   FB-M, p. 192.

9   Dr Luther Cloud, interviewed by Russell Davies, c. 1980 (private collection). There is some uncertainty about exactly when Dr Cloud made his appearance.

10 Ibid.

11 Buddy Tate, interviewed by Russell Davies (private collection).

12 Interview with Patricia Willard for Rutgers Jazz Oral History Project. Quoted in FB-M, p. 213.

13 Maurice Cullaz, 'Mon Ami, Lester Young', *Jazz Hot*, May 1959.

14 See note 9.

15 James Jones, introduction to *Jazz People* by Dan Morgenstern (New York: Harry N. Abrams, 1976), p. 16.

Chapter 13

1   Allen Ginsberg, *Howl and Other Poems* (San Francisco: City Lights, 1956), *Composed on the Tongue* (Bolinas: Grey Fox Press, 1980).

2   The exception is Paul Quinichette, who deliberately set out to reproduce Lester's style as closely as possible, and became known for a while as the 'Vice-Prez'.

3   See, for example, the long interview with Bill Triglia in FB-M, p. 184.

4   *Miles: The Autobiography* (New York: Simon & Schuster, 1989), p. 89.

5   Gunther Schuller, *The Swing Era: The Development of Jazz, 1930–1945* (New York, Oxford University Press, 1989), p. 554.

6   Philip Larkin, *All What Jazz? A Record Diary* (London: Faber & Faber, rev. edn, 1985), p. 170.

select discography

The following list of recordings covers the whole of Lester Young's recording career. It does not include everything he recorded, but I believe all the most important material is here. It has proved impossible to avoid overlapping and duplication, but I have tried to keep this to a minimum. I have added all known film and television items available on DVD. It cannot be guaranteed that these particular editions will be available.

All jazz material released by Verve Records is now available for downloading. See www.classicsandjazz.co.uk

CDs

The Lester Young Story (4-CD box set). Proper Records PROPERBOX 8.
An excellent anthology of Lester's recorded work, from the very beginning (October 1936) to September 1949. The 84 tracks include a good selection of recordings with Basie, Billie Holiday, the Kansas City Six and Seven, and Lester's own bands on the Savoy and Aladdin labels. The best possible introduction.

Count Basie – Original American Decca Recordings (3-CD box set). GRP records GRD 3611-2.
All 63 tracks recorded under Basie's first recording contract, featuring Prez in many early classics, including 'Swingin' the Blues', 'Every Tub', 'Jumpin' At The Woodside', 'Jive At Five', etc.

Count Basie – America's #1 Band (4-CD box set). Columbia Legacy 512892-2.
Although this collection contains much non-Lester material, the 90 tracks do include his debut recording session in full, plus Basie's Bad Boys, the Kansas City Seven, the best of his Columbia recordings with Basie's full band, plus live broadcasts from the Famous Door, Savoy Ballroom, etc. These contain the only surviving recordings of Billie singing with the Basie band.

A Lester Young Story. Jazz Archives No. 48.
A nicely chosen single-CD selection containing 22 tracks from the years 1936–1940, with Count Basie, Billie Holiday and the Kansas City Six and Seven.

Pres & Billie Complete (double-CD set). Jazz Factory JFCD 22832.
Everything from the great late-30s sessions.

Kansas City Swing. Definitive Records DRCD11118.
Complete small band recordings on Commodore (1938), Signature (1943) and Keynote (1944) – 21 sublime tracks altogether.

Count Basie: Lang-Worth Transcriptions. Soundies SCD 4128.
Rare studio recordings from Lester's second Basie period, featuring many excellent solos.

Count Basie & his Orchestra (1944). Circle 60.
A complete live-broadcast set from the Hotel Lincoln's 'Blue Room'.

Lester Young Savoy Masters. Definitive Records DRCD 111151.
Lester's recordings (both pre- and post-Army) for the Savoy label, including the superb 'Ghost Of A Chance' (1944) and the fruits of the great session of 28 June 1949.

Jammin' The Blues. Definitive Records DRCD 11117.
Everything recorded by Norman Granz for the soundtrack of the film, including music which didn't make it into the final version. The second half of the disc contains live concert recordings from 1946.

Complete Aladdin Recordings of Lester Young. Blue Note CDP 7243 8 32787 2 5.
A double-CD set which starts with the fascinating four 1942 tracks with Nat Cole and Red Callender and takes in all Lester's Philo-Aladdin records, including the classic 'DB Blues'. Forty tracks altogether, including one previously unissued.

Sarah Vaughan / Lester Young – One Night Stand. Blue Note 7243 8 32139 2 4.
A 1947 concert at New York Town Hall. *Down Beat* magazine panned Lester's performance, although it's hard to understand why. He and the band sound in excellent form.

Lester Young Live at the Royal Roost 1948. Jazz Anthology 550092.
New York's 'Royal Roost' was a club strongly associated with the latest developments in jazz. Prez was one of few representatives of his generation to appear there regularly, and these bright, sharp performances with his band of 'kiddies' show how at-home he was in bebop surroundings.

The Complete Lester Young Studio Sesssions on Verve. Verve 314 547 087-2.
A huge, eight-CD compendium of everything recorded by Lester for Norman Granz's Verve label and its forerunners, Mercury, Clef and Norgran. Essentially, this is the musical record of the last ten years of Prez's life, although it actually begins with a stray session with Nat Cole and Buddy Rich from 1946. The best and the worst of those years are all here – from the wonderfully delicate interplay with John Lewis, through the joyful reunion with Teddy Wilson and the hilarious 'Takes Two To Tango' episode, to the final, gasping notes in Paris in March 1959. The package also contains the original tape recordings of the interviews with François Postif and Chris Albertson.

Lester Young 1947-1951. Classics 1247.
Lester Young 1951-1952. Classics 1325.
These two CDs contain all Lester's studio recordings with John Lewis, and some of his best early-50s work with pianists Hank Jones and Oscar Peterson.

Lester Young with the Oscar Peterson Trio. Verve 521 451-2.
This is the 1952 session containing Lester's odd but endearing 'Takes Two To Tango' vocal. His playing on the whole session gives the lie to those critics who write off his post-Army period as one long decline.

The Jazz Giants '56. Verve 825 672-2.
Pres & Teddy. Verve 831 270-2.
Recorded on successive days in January 1956, these two impressive sessions find Lester reunited with Teddy Wilson and other contemporaries and mark a high point in the up-and-down progress of his life in his final decade.

Lester Young In Washington DC, 1956 (Vols 1–5). Original Jazz Classics OJC 782 / 881 / 901 / 1043 / 1051.
Lester's playing on these live sessions at a Washington nightclub is quite enthralling. All the hesitancy and weakness that beset him at other times is simply brushed aside and replaced by inspired eloquence. All five sets

are superb, but Vol. 2 is perhaps the best of all, with towering versions of 'Lester Leaps In' and 'These Foolish Things'.

Laughin' To Keep From Cryin'. Verve 543 301-2.
Little more than a year before his death, weak and audibly struggling, Lester produces a few gems against all the odds. Especially moving is his clarinet on 'They Can't Take That Away From Me'.

DVD

Great Performances. Idem DVD 1057.
Contains the whole of *Jammin' The Blues* (plus audio tracks of unused music), together with five numbers by a 1950 Jazz At The Philharmonic group, featuring Prez alongside Charlie Parker, Harry 'Sweets' Edison, Ella Fitzgerald and others. Also contains footage of Charlie Parker, Dizzy Gillespie and Miles Davis.

The Sound Of Jazz. MVD Music Video DJ-108.
The complete CBS TV broadcast of December 1958, in which Lester and Billie appear together for the last time. Also featuring Coleman Hawkins, Count Basie and others who figure in Lester Young's story.

index

Compositions and published articles are indicated by quote marks. Entries in italic indicate albums or books. Page numbers in italic indicate illustrated material. 'L' indicates Lester Young.